THE COLLEGE DROPOUT
SCANDAL

THE COLLEGE DROPOUT SCANDAL

DAVID KIRP

OXFORD
UNIVERSITY PRESS

OXFORD
UNIVERSITY PRESS

Oxford University Press is a department of the University of Oxford. It furthers
the University's objective of excellence in research, scholarship, and education
by publishing worldwide. Oxford is a registered trade mark of Oxford University
Press in the UK and certain other countries.

Published in the United States of America by Oxford University Press
198 Madison Avenue, New York, NY 10016, United States of America.

© David Kirp 2019

Library of Congress Cataloging-in-Publication Data
Names: Kirp, David, author.
Title: The college dropout scandal / David Kirp.
Description: New York, NY : Oxford University Press, [2019] |
Includes bibliographical references.
Identifiers: LCCN 2018038832 (print) | LCCN 2019006141 (ebook) |
ISBN 9780190862220 (updf) | ISBN 9780190862237 (epub) |
ISBN 9780190862213 (hardcover)
Subjects: LCSH: College dropouts—United States—Prevention.
Classification: LCC LC148.15 (ebook) | LCC LC148.15 .K57 2019 (print) |
DDC 378.1/6913—dc23
LC record available at https://lccn.loc.gov/2018038832

1 3 5 7 9 8 6 4 2

Printed by Sheridan Books, Inc., United States of America

TABLE OF CONTENTS

THE COLLEGE DROPOUT
SCANDAL

INTRODUCTION
The Scandal and the Solutions

David Laude, until recently the graduation rate champion at the University of Texas, was musing about why undergraduates drop out. "Students try their best, but there are all these evil things that can happen, from a bad test to a grandmother with a heart attack to a breakup with a girlfriend. The only way you can save that kid is constant vigilance, just watching for those moments—before they get sucked down, they're pulled up and saved."

"Here's the story that makes me angriest, because this was on my watch. This was an African-American male from the inner city, a first-generation college student with a 1350 or 1400 on his SAT—the kind of kid that Harvard takes in a heartbeat, with a full ride. It was a miracle we were going to get this guy. He wanted to be an engineer, wear UT orange, all that. We were going to help this kid out, put him into a six-week summer program, all paid for, so he could take calculus early."

"It was all looking good, everything's fine, he's a rock star. But the night before his first calculus test, his girlfriend calls to break up with him. He does what every self-respecting male does, he stays on the phone with her all night long, begging her not to break up with him. Then, distraught, he takes his first calculus test and fails it. He calls his mother on the phone, and tells her that he's failed the first test, and she gets in the car, drives here, picks him up, puts him in the car, takes him home, withdraws him from school, and says 'I told you so, they don't care.'"

"This is a true story. What I said to those people who ran that success program: this is on us. That kid should have known that he could have come to one of us and said, 'I can't take this test,' but he didn't know, and that's why he's gone. All it takes is that one little tiny thing like that, and then they're not here. So when I think about whether or not [students graduate], it's because of the hundreds of times that they faced this evil, and someone saved them."[1]

Writing in *Femsplain*, Meghan Kehoe—"master of sass," she calls herself—tells a similar tale from her vantage as a dropout. "I tried making an appointment with one of the school counselors early on—not only to discuss my lack of a financial plan, but to discuss how I felt like I was drowning. How fantastic I'd become at faking it, how I had almost everyone fooled. Sometimes, I could even fool myself. The morning of my appointment, the counselor called and cancelled. I took it as a sign from the universe. A big ol' middle-finger courtesy of some brand of wicked karma that wanted me to be miserable forever."[2]

A Google search for stories about the lives of dropouts turns up almost nothing. Geoffrey Widdison, himself a decade out of college, who describes himself as "engineer, reader, thinker, dreamer," explains why. "We never hear those stories because they're so ubiquitous as to be boring. It's like asking for stories of someone who started up a rock band that went nowhere or ran for political office against all odds and lost. Talk to any musician or political activist and you'll get a hundred stories like that, and they all sound the same."

"I have several friends and relatives who dropped out of college. Every one of them ended up working low-end jobs, usually in spurts between being unemployed. Some patched together basically decent, if poor, lives for themselves. Others completely lapsed into hopelessness and depression. Nothing much in there to make for an interesting story."[3]

Washington Post reporter Kavitha Cardoza zeroed in on one such student, Christopher Feaster. Christopher lived in a homeless shelter during his high school years, and while homeless students face long odds against graduating, he was an academic whiz kid, "the poster child for grit." He headed to Michigan State with a full ride, the first in his family to go to college, only to drop out a year later. It was "an insanely big change," Christopher recalls. He had gone to an all-black high school in Washington, DC, and now he was surrounded by white students. He had to take remedial math, which left him wondering whether he was good enough to be at the university. He floundered academically, but no one reached out to him. He dropped out after failing his finals. Three years later, Christopher was struggling with homelessness and having a hard time getting a full-time job. "He desperately wants to go back to college," Cardoza writes, "but without a scholarship, he'd have to take out loans. 'I don't think that's a good idea,' he says. 'Not for me right now.' He's also afraid of 'failing again.' "

When students—especially poor, minority, or first-gen students, whom I'll refer to collectively as *"new-gen" students*—drop out, the feeling that they're to blame for having failed, that they're not "college material," affects not just themselves but those close to them as well. "Every [new-gen] student has a story of a cousin, a sibling, a friend, a neighbor who went to college but had to drop out. And that is what a lot of people use as a reason for students not to go."[4]

The Illusion of Mobility

Higher education is billed as the ticket of admission to America's middle class. That's true for students who earn a bachelor's degree—their lifetime earnings will be nearly $1 million more than those with only a high school diploma, and the gap keeps widening as more employers demand a university credential.[5]

But the contention that college is the engine of social mobility is false advertising for the 34 million Americans over twenty-five—that's more than 10 percent of the entire US population—who have some college credits but dropped out before receiving a diploma. Many of them are actually worse off economically than if they hadn't started college. While they earn a little more than those who never went beyond high school, they leave college with a pile of debt, but without the chance to secure the high-paying jobs to pay it off that a degree would open up. Dropouts are nearly twice as likely to be unemployed as college grads, and they are four times more likely to default on student loans, thus wrecking their credit and shrinking their career options.[6]

The American Institutes for Research calculates that the cost of dropping out, measured by lost earnings, is $3.8 billion, and that's just for a single year and a single class of students.[7] But dollars-and-cents calculations tell only a fraction of the story. A college education gives students the intellectual capital to tackle high-skill jobs, as well as the social capital to make the connections and build the networks that can lead to success. What's more, *New York Times* columnist David Leonhardt points out that "as the [income] disparity widens, it is doing so in ways that go beyond income, from home-ownership to marriage to retirement. Education has become a dividing line that affects how Americans vote, the likelihood that they will own a home and their geographic mobility. Educational gaps in life expectancy and health status are growing too."[8]

Fewer than 60 percent of college freshmen graduate in six years, two years beyond the norm, and that rate has barely changed during the past decade.[9] Community college students are meant to earn an associate degree in two years, but even after having been in school for six years, fewer than 40 percent have graduated or transferred to a university.[10] The United States ranks nineteenth in graduation rates among the twenty-eight countries studied by the Organisation for Economic Co-operation and Development (OECD), putting the country on a par with Lithuania and Slovenia.[11] A company that had so much trouble hanging on to its customers would go out of business.

Statistics can be numbing, the stuff of policy wonkery, but bear with me—the deeper you dive into these numbers, the bleaker the picture that emerges. Public universities graduate fewer than half their students and less than a quarter of those who enroll in for-profits like the University of Phoenix earn a bachelor's degree.[12] If these schools were held to the same standard as our high schools, 85 percent of them would be branded dropout factories.[13]

Some students leave school because of money woes, and others realize that college isn't right for them.[14] But many, like Christopher Feaster, depart because the institution hasn't given them the we-have-your-back support they need.

The fact that 40 percent of college freshmen never make it to commencement is higher education's dirty little secret, a dereliction of duty that has gotten too little public attention. When Richard Arum and Josipa Roksa, in

Academically Adrift, a widely read account of undergraduate life, surveyed more than 2,300 students, they discovered widespread disaffection with their school and inattention to academics. The typical student, they found, studies about seventeen hours a week, about half as much as their peers studied in the early 1960s.

Strikingly, the universities didn't seem to care. "Faculty and administrators, working to meet multiple and at times competing demands, too rarely focus on either improving instruction or demonstrating gains in student learning."[15] The priority, for many college presidents, is getting freshmen in the door and tuition dollars in the bank. Meanwhile, professors go about their business, inattentive to the problem—ask most professors about how many students depart their institution and you're likely to get puzzled looks and an off-the-mark guesstimate.[16]

No one is held accountable for this sorry state of affairs. Nobody gets fired because students are dropping out.

A growing number of states have tied funding to graduation rates. Though this pressure tactic is tempting to politicians, such financial incentives are blunt policy instruments that may backfire, making it harder for poor students to get admitted to college because they are worse bets to graduate. A Century Foundation report argues that focusing entirely on outcomes is reinforcing disparities between institutional haves and have-nots, while failing to move the needle on completion. "Students can be derailed from graduating for many different reasons, including a lack of academic preparation or money. Colleges with ample resources can readily address those needs to raise graduation rates, but schools with limited means often struggle."[17]

"We have met the enemy and he is us"—Pogo's immortal line is dead on. Universities are not powerless to change this situation, but many of them take a hands-off approach. Administrators and professors who cling to the raft of high standards and low expectations contend that these students have had their chance. They've blown it—case closed. "Our job is to give you an opportunity; your job is to take advantage of it. If you don't, oh, well."[18]

"Give us better students and we'll graduate more of them," the apologists cry, but that excuse doesn't wash. The graduation rate at universities whose students look alike on paper varies by as many as 20 percentage points. To take one example, about 20 percent of Chicago State University's students earn a bachelor's degree, while more than twice as many graduate from

North Carolina Central University, which enrolls students with similar academic credentials.[19]

The new-gen students have the most to gain from having a college degree. Stanford economist Raj Chetty and his colleagues at the Economic Opportunity Project identified a handful of universities, among them the City College of New York and Cal State-Los Angeles, that are making good on the pledge of economic mobility, catapulting students from poor families into the middle class. But these schools are the decided exceptions. Here's a set-your-hair-on-fire statistic—more than three-quarters of students whose families are in the top 25 percent earning bracket earn a bachelor's degree, compared to barely *one-tenth* as many from the bottom 25 percent.[20] Higher education doesn't simply maintain social class distinctions. It widens the chasm between rich and poor.

More than a third of undergraduates are the first in their family to go to college. Unlike their middle-class classmates, there's no one they can rely on to explain how to cope with the stresses of college life. They would benefit greatly if their professors, counselors, and advisers were easy to reach, as they are at top schools, but on most campuses this kind of mentoring is a luxury.[21] Advisers rank near the bottom on most universities' priority list—in big public universities, an adviser may be assigned upward of 1,000 students, and individual students become merely statistical artifacts. This inattention helps to explain why white students graduate at a rate 10 percentage points higher than Latinos, and 20 percentage points higher than black students.[22]

Education Trust, a Washington, DC, nonprofit, flagged twenty-six institutions where black and Latino students are at least as likely to graduate as their classmates, but comparable schools are doing much worse. For instance, the high school GPAs and SAT scores of University of California-Riverside undergraduates are the same as students at the University of Illinois-Chicago, but 30 percent fewer black students earn a bachelor's degree at UIC.[23]

Recipients of Pell Grants, the federal financial aid program for students from poor and working-class families—a third of the college population—also fare badly. Their six-year graduation rate is 20 percent lower than students who aren't getting this subsidy. As with overall graduation rates, there's a yawning gap between the best- and worst-performing colleges. A 2017 Brookings Institution report identifies fourteen universities, among them UMass Boston and CUNY York College, where the graduation rate for Pell recipients is higher than for non-Pell students. At the other end of the spectrum, the same report fingers the University of Akron for a hall-of-shame award. There, 9 percent of Pell Grant recipients graduate in six years (you read that number right), versus 70 percent of the rest of the students. The situation is nearly as dire for Akron's African American students, who have a 13 percent graduation rate.

WHAT WORKS

The dropout problem could be solved in a New York minute if diplomas were handed out to every undergraduate who sticks around for four years. That's a preposterous proposal, one that's worthy of a Jonathan Swift satire, but a Cal State English professor actually recommended something similar to his colleagues. Because black and Latino students live on-the-precipice lives, he argued, simply showing up for class should earn them a B.

Solutions to the dropout crisis need not be so fanciful, for every college administrator with a pulse knows the tools that have been proven to remedy the dropout problem. They don't cost a fortune and they don't require a genius to make them work. We'll examine each of these tools in Chapter 1 and dig deeper at the universities we'll visit in later chapters.

Here's the in-a-nutshell summary.

Information that identifies top-flight colleges that talented students from poor families didn't realize were within reach helps them make better choices.

Text message *nudges* prod students into starting, and staying in, college.

The voluminous amount of information a university collects about its undergraduates can be parsed, using *data analytics*, to anticipate which freshmen are likely to need help. This number-crunching also enables an institution to spot those who are having trouble early, enabling advisers to corral them before their problems ripen into crises.

Brief *experiences*, rooted in psychological insight, which promote a sense of belonging and a growth mindset make students more resilient when confronted with the predictable setbacks of undergraduate life.

Revamping make-or-break classes—remedial math, reading, and writing—the downfall for millions of students—substantially lowers the number of failing grades.

Building connections across the community college–university divide gives students in two-year schools a direct route to a bachelor's degree—a clear incentive to pursue their education—as well as providing universities with well-prepared upperclassmen.

These strategies work for one basic reason. *They enable students to recognize that they are full-fledged members of a community that takes them seriously, as individuals, rather than members of an impersonal bureaucracy that batch-processes them like Perdue chickens.*

During my campus visits I asked students why they were enthusiastic about their college. I kept hearing the same answer—*they have our back.*

For more than half a century, UCLA's Higher Education Research Institute has surveyed more than 15 million students at over 1,900 colleges. The bottom line: "The more students are academically and socially engaged with other people on campus, the more likely (other things being equal) that they will stay and graduate from college."[24] A recent study of nearly 7,000 students on thirty-four campuses reached the same conclusion. "Students' perception of the degree to which the institution was supportive of their academic, personal and social needs was the most powerful predictor of increased academic competence."

In short, *the more students believe that they belong, the better they do academically.* The reverse is also true—without this kind of engagement, "the social loneliness that follows often leads to withdrawal."[25]

"A revolution appears to be sweeping the campuses of the nation's colleges and universities, and it is based on a simple credo: The success of an institution and the success of its students are inseparable."[26] It is sad, and telling, that three professors who have spent their careers studying the doings of universities believe that putting students first is a revolutionary idea.

Unfortunately, they're right. Some universities, as we'll see, have made the changes necessary to turn this credo into reality. There, more students are graduating, and the graduation gap is closing or has disappeared entirely. But making significant changes, like revamping big-enrollment courses or investing heavily in just-in-time advising, demands a leader with the courage to act, as well as the talent to create a compelling vision and develop a sense of urgency among campus constituents. Leaders like this are in short supply.

College presidents aren't generally known for their bravery. Instead, they wax eloquent about the imperative of student success; or invoke buzzwords like "data analytics," as if rhetoric could substitute for action; or fantasize about quick fixes; or launch ill-considered pilot projects; or gather mountains of data that sits unused.

"I'm appalled that so many universities continue to engage in practices known to be, at best, modestly effective," Mark Becker, the president of Georgia State, tells me, and when nothing comes of those efforts, the administrators blame the tools, not themselves. They are driven by the desire to enhance their institution's prestige, as defined by its standing in the *U.S. News* pecking order. This fixation on status explains why scholarships are increasingly awarded on the basis of students' academic credentials, not their financial need.[27]

A college president has many competing priorities—raising money, placating lawmakers, wooing donors, managing crises, and the like—and rarely does the dropout problem make the cut. "Few institutions take student retention seriously," says Syracuse emeritus professor Vincent Tinto, the author of *Completing College*. "Most treat it as one more item to add to the list of issues to be addressed." [28]

"We're convinced that serving underserved students is an important thing to push out into the higher education world," Michael Crow, the president of Arizona State, a break-the-mold university that enrolls more than 80,000 students, asserts. You might think Crow was stating the obvious, since higher education is sold as the glide path to the middle class, but this is not how most colleges operate. "The graduation rate is something we can have a tremendous amount of influence over, and we had to make a conscious decision to do this."

The status quo exerts a mighty appeal, and the prospect of doing things differently invariably brings opponents out of the woodwork. "There's no reason to expect presidents to be change agents," Josh Wyner, the executive director of the College Excellence Program at the Aspen Institute, points out, "especially if that change is risky and not necessary to preserve the 'quality' of their institutions, measured by traditional definitions of enrollment, buildings, and prestige."

When I asked Tim Renick, the student success czar at Georgia State, whether institutional inertia explains why so many universities weren't tackling the dropout problem, he replied that "it is more than inertia—it is structural. I visit lots of campuses. They invite me because they see the changes made at Georgia State and want similar successes. But when I get to campus and explain how we centralized advising, to make it better, I hear they could never do that because the Dean of X wouldn't support it, and the Dean of X is supported by the trustees. When I talk about junking lectures in math, and making the courses more interactive, I hear that the faculty senate would never go against the chair of math to enact such changes."

Yet unless university leaders are up for the challenge—unless they regard student success not as a risky business but as a moral imperative—the dropout problem won't be solved.[29] "It's almost as if students require a winning lottery ticket to have a better shot of succeeding in college," says Brad Phillips, president of the Institute for Evidence-Based Change. "What would it look like if colleges made a real commitment to scale a few high-impact, research-based programs?"[30]

The six strategies that I summarized offer a solid starting point for a university that's determined to keep its students in school, but there's no one-size-fits-all formula. The logjams that undergraduates encounter on their way to graduation—the courses they need for their major but can't get into, the bureaucratic rigmarole they encounter, the bottomless pit of remedial math into which they slip—must be identified before solutions can emerge, and these vary from school to school. A university's culture—its shared values, history, and identity—exerts a powerful force. Budgetary realities affect what's doable.

At the annual meeting of the American Council on Education a few years back, Freeman Hrabowski III, the long-time president of the University of Maryland, Baltimore County, exhorted his colleagues not to adopt a "what can you expect?" attitude toward poor and minority students, but instead to focus on "what they can become." Hrabowski's deeds match his words—UMBC produces more black bachelor's degree recipients who go to complete MD-PhDs than any other college in the country.

Though a handful of hypercompetitive colleges, like Amherst, which we'll visit later, and Vassar have made a point of admitting more poor and working-class students, their efforts are just a thimblefull in the ocean of need. And among the elite schools, these are rarities. Here's a you've-got-to-be-kidding fact: *at thirty-eight elite colleges, including five in the Ivy League—Dartmouth, Princeton, Yale, Penn, and Brown—more students come from the top 1 percent of the income scale than from the entire bottom 60 percent.*[31]

It's at the outsized state universities and community colleges, the mass-education institutions that educate nearly 80 percent of undergraduates, where the dropout problem is most severe and where the need for action is greatest.[32] If you don't know much about some of campuses we'll be looking at, or if you think that institutions like these can't deliver a decent education, you're in for a whopping surprise. Consider the University of Central Florida, the second-biggest public institution in the country, which justifiably refers to itself as the best university no one has heard of; or its neighbor, Valencia College, named the nation's top community college by the Aspen Institute, where the quality of teaching rivals that of any school; or Long Beach State, which must be doing something right, since it has the nation's seventh-most applicants, about twice as many as Harvard.

At these universities, and others like them, Hrabowski's admonition embodies the implicit mission statement. The graduation rate keeps increasing, and the new-gen students are catching up to, or in some cases exceeding, their classmates. These schools tailor the known-to-work strategies to fit their circumstances, while including home-grown ideas in their bag of tricks. Each takes a somewhat different approach to engaging its students, and it's these differences—variations on the theme of promoting students' sense of belonging—that we'll focus on.[33] By showing what can be accomplished without making a herculean effort, or having Hercules at the helm, these accounts are meant to prod institutions with scandalous track records into action.

1

MOVING THE NEEDLE ON STUDENT SUCCESS
Strategies All Colleges Can Use

The late Justice Antonin Scalia was a provocateur par excellence, well known for shooting from the lip. Case in point: *Fisher v. University of Texas.*

During oral argument in this 2013 affirmative action case, Scalia noted that "there are those who contend that it does not benefit African Americans to get them into the University of Texas, where they do not do well, as opposed to having them go to a less-advanced school, a slower-track school where they do well." The Justice left no room for doubt where he stood. "Most of the black scientists in this country don't come from schools like the University of Texas.... They come from lesser schools where they do not feel that they're being pushed ahead in classes that are too fast for them." Then he administered the *coup de grace.* "I'm just not impressed by the fact that the University of Texas may have fewer [blacks]. Maybe it ought to have fewer."[1]

Scalia was inelegantly referring to what's known as the "mismatch" theory, which holds that minority students admitted to top-of-the-ladder universities find themselves over their head, academically, and fare worse than they would have at second-tier institutions. Most academics disagree, pointing out that these undergraduates are far more likely to graduate than if they had gone to less prestigious schools."[2]

If you are serious about combating the dropout crisis, concentrate on the new-gen students who are "under-matched" in their choice of college. "Chase them down, inspire them, hold their hands, push their families, cut some deals—do whatever it takes," argued Clifford Adelman, the longtime doyen of research at the US Department of Education.[3]

Wealthy parents do their damnedest to secure a slot at a highly competitive school for their less-than-Einstein offspring. But many high achievers from new-gen families—the poor, minority, and first-generation college-goers—don't even consider applying to these places.[4] Often there is no one in their family who knows, at first hand, the long-run implications of choosing among colleges. Without sound advice from guidance counselors, who are scarce on the ground, or visits to their high schools from college admissions officers, they don't know that, with their credentials, they would almost certainly be admitted to a better university. And because those schools have more scholarship money available, in many cases these students would receive a financial aid package so generous that it would actually save them money. Scared off by the sticker price, they wind up at community colleges and less selective institutions.

Since the higher-ranked schools do a better job of making sure that their students earn a degree, under-matching explains nearly 10 percent of the graduation gap between new-gen and traditional college students.[5] It's also a big reason why nearly three-quarters of the students at top-ranked universities are the scions of families in the top quarter of the income bracket, while students from families in the bottom quarter make up only 3 percent.[6] So few poor students enroll in these schools that well-off students with weak high grades and test scores—the "dumb rich," Brookings economist Stephen Burd calls them—often wind up with the most scholarship money. "There's a premium, now, on being wealthy."[7]

INFORMATION CHANGES MINDS

Economists appreciate the value of information in making informed choices, whether it's picking a restaurant or buying a car. The economic model of decision-making works for selecting a college as well, as Caroline

Hoxby at Stanford, Christopher Avery at Harvard, and Sarah Turner at the University of Virginia have shown. These economists tracked 40,000 seniors who scored in the top 10 percent on the SAT or ACT, and whose families' earnings fell in the bottom third of the income distribution. Most of these students were sent packets telling them how to find schools that matched their interests, with information about those colleges' academic offerings and graduation rates, as well as estimates of what it would actually cost them to attend a variety of schools. The control group didn't get any of this material.

The impact was far bigger than the researchers anticipated. Those who received the packet were 78 percent more likely to be accepted by a major university, where the overall graduation rate was 15 percent higher than at less selective institutions. When the information was accompanied by a waiver of application fees, the impact on where students applied was even greater. These students also knew more about whether the academic programs of the schools they considered were a good fit for them.

The intervention cost less than fifteen dollars a student. Every dollar invested returned at least four dollars in benefits, and this doesn't take into account the ripple effect on classmates from these high schools who learn that they too can aim higher.[8]

It would cost a pittance to get students like these the material they need to make smarter decisions about where to go to college. No college is likely to act on its own, since the benefits would be spread among many schools, but a higher education consortium, government agency, or foundation could tackle the assignment. Not only would these students likely get a better education, they'd have a much better shot at graduating.

More recently, high-achieving, low-income high school seniors were encouraged to apply to the University of Michigan with the promise of four years of a tuition-free education. Almost all of U of M students with a similar background were already receiving the same aid package, so the offer cost the university nothing. But in a 2018 study, Michigan economist Susan Dynarski and her colleagues found that a personalized letter, signed by the university president and sent to these students, as well as their parents and counselors, made all the difference. More than twice as many students notified of this opportunity applied to the university than their peers who didn't receive this information, and more than twice as many enrolled at Ann Arbor. The effect was to halve the income gap in college choices among top-in-the-class students; what's more, those students were much less likely to drop out of college than their classmates with comparable high school records who went to less prestigious schools. There's every reason why flagship universities in other states should take the same approach.[9]

THE POWER OF NUDGES

The first step in helping students graduate is ensuring that they get to campus at the start of their freshmen year.

You might assume that, having gone to the considerable trouble of completing an application, students would jump at the opportunity to go to the university of their choice. But a sizable number—as many as 40 percent in some urban school districts—who have been accepted never show up. Some decide not to enroll because of a change of heart—the realization that college isn't for them—or a change of circumstances that keeps them tethered to their families. Often, though, the explanation is that they don't know what steps they must take once they're accepted.

Unlike their well-off peers, who benefit from an elaborate support network, these adolescents are left to their own devices. They are understandably daunted by having to navigate the passage between high school and college—completing financial aid forms, submitting final grades, picking courses, and signing up for orientation. The phenomenon is known as "summer melt," and it's a big reason why well-intentioned attempts to enroll more poor students fall short.

Counseling might well narrow this gap. But counselors, especially in poor high schools, already have oversize caseloads—as many as 1,000 students— and little if any time to focus on those who have already been admitted to college.[10]

Economists Ben Castleman, at the University of Virginia, and Lindsay Page, at the University of Pittsburgh, have devised a light-touch approach— a text-messaging campaign directed at potentially vulnerable students during the summer before they start school. The messages are customized to remind them of the deadlines set by their intended college and tell them where they can find help if they're stumped by the paperwork.[11]

Texts are how teenagers communicate—nearly two-thirds of them send texts daily, rather than talk on their phones or reply to an email—and it's sensible to connect with them on their go-to device. "Hi, Alex!" a typical message might say. "Have you chosen your courses yet? Deadline is 8/15 . . . Need help? Text back to speak w/ an adviser." Georgia State University, which tested the nudge approach in 2017, reduced summer melt by more than 20 percent, adding about 400 students to the freshman class.

"The educational landscape requires students to navigate a series of complex decisions and complicated processes. These are likely to be particularly difficult for economically disadvantaged students, and in turn the behavioral bottlenecks are likely to worsen the existing inequalities," Castleman tells me. "The biggest impact is among the poorest and first-generation college-going students. We're providing them with the same kinds of nudges and encouragement that middle-class parents are doing for their college-bound kids."

The cost of texting and counseling? Less than seven dollars a student. Deliver this assistance to high school seniors nationwide and hundreds of thousands more poor students will make it to college. Ben Castleman dreams big: "Can we go from 50,000 to 500,000—to five million?"

Summer melt isn't the only use to which nudges can be put. "Winston, where do you come from?" queries a student at Winston-Salem State, a historically black university in North Carolina. Another classmate asks: "Have you ever been in love?" But Winston isn't a person. It's the happy face the university has put on an artificial intelligence (AI) system that messages students to keep them focused once the school year begins.

"We're a lot less transactional than we used to be. We're reaching students where they are, not just hoping they're where they are supposed to be," explains Joel Lee, the dean who's responsible for keeping students on track. That's why this AI system was so appealing. The students weren't reading their emails, and making personal phone calls was too expensive. A startup called AdmitHub promoted this technology as a way to enhance back-and-forth communication between the college and its students. Winston-Salem signed up in 2017.

With more than 1,400 questions and answers stockpiled in the system, many of them added in response to students' queries, the AI system can respond instantaneously to almost anything a student wants to know. And while it provides information, it also gets students involved by asking questions like "Do you know the deadline for the Pell Grant paperwork?"

Even though the students are well aware that Winston is a chat-bot, they assign it human characteristics. "They can ask any question without feeling they're being judged—questions they wouldn't ask a person because they fear they would sound stupid," Joel Lee told me. "Can we date?" a girl asks, the real-life version of the 2013 hit movie *Her*, about a lonely writer who falls in love with an operating system designed to satisfy his every need. Winston has a ready reply: "I'm not sure a robot and a human would make good dates."

This jokey personalization is one reason the chat-bot isn't an eat-your-spinach nag. Joel Lee believes it deserves at least part of the credit for the fact that, in 2018, 2 percent more freshmen returned for the spring semester than the previous year. At a cost of less than $50,000, it's a no-brainer investment.

THE CHRYSTAL BALL

A decade ago, Georgia State University faced a massive problem—two-thirds of its students were dropping out. Hundreds of big public universities find themselves in the same boat, but rather than whining about the quality of its students or the skimpiness of its budget, as other schools do, GSU decided to act. As we'll see in the next chapter, it analyzed a decade's worth of grades to spot the biggest roadblocks, then built an early warning system to catch these problems before they morphed into full-blown crises.

Dissecting vast amounts of information—data-mining, it's called—has been widely used outside academe since the 1990s.[12] In 2002, when an upstart named Billy Beane, then the general manager of the Oakland A's, introduced statistically sophisticated gauges of player performance into the tradition-laden world of major league baseball, the grandees scoffed. His rigorous analysis of millions of data-points showed that a player's on-base percentage and slugging percentage were better predictors of offensive prowess than speed and batting average, the criteria general managers had always relied on. Using those metrics, he signed players, passed over by other teams, at bargain-basement prices. The derision ceased when the A's, despite having one of the major league's smallest budgets, twice made it to the playoffs. *Moneyball* became a box office smash and a baseball staple.[13]

The real moneyball is played with the greatest intensity where the big money is, in the private sector. Companies like Amazon, United Airlines, and Uber possess the know-how to juggle prices in a matter of seconds, depending on demand—check the price of a flight more than once and the cost goes up—and when you are put on hold, your place in the queue ("you are number ninety-nine; your wait time is approximately one hour") depends on whether, according to the algorithm, you're a "high value" customer. Audi offers a better deal to a customer who, the data indicates, is likely to switch to Mercedes-Benz than someone who will probably stick with Audi. By analyzing patterns in masses of complaints, United Healthcare can adjust its practices and anticipate how many customers it's likely to lose. Big data tools are used to operate Google's self-driving car, and big data algorithms make split-second decisions about buying and selling stocks.

In a well-known case, the father of a teenage girl started receiving coupons from Target for baby products. When he complained to Target, he found out that, by tracking his daughter's purchases, the company could predict that she was pregnant before he had an inkling. "We knew that if we could identify them in their second trimester, there's a good chance we could capture them for years," explains a Target statistician. "As soon as we get them buying diapers from us, they're going to start buying everything else too."[14]

Public health officials were quick to grasp the life-saving potential of big data. Medical records, combined with information gleaned from social media, can predict flu outbreaks. Statewide electronic prescription-monitoring databases identify patients who doctor-shop for opioids. Health apps turn a smartphone into a biomedical research device. And population-based health tools can spot those at risk of developing diabetes or congestive heart failure.[15]

As with many tools developed for the corporate world, higher education came late to the party, but data analytics has become de rigueur. It's easy to understand why. Admissions officers haven't known the best places to hunt for likely prospects.[16] Professors haven't known which students are lagging until midterm exam results are in, and by then they have fallen far behind their classmates. Administrators haven't known that a student is in hot water until a D appears on the transcript.

Big data promises to fill in the blanks by rooting decisions in science, not hunch.

Advisers can reach out to students when signs of trouble first appear, rather than waiting for them to show up at their door. Administrators can use digital dashboards that highlight students who are struggling. They can locate, and do something about, the bottlenecks that keep students from progressing, like the math class, required for graduation, that many students fail, or a shortage of seats in a course that students must take for their major.

Because data-mining has shown that students who work on campus are less likely to drop out than those with burger-flipping jobs, administrators can comb students' records, looking for those who are eligible for federally subsidized work-study jobs and finding them less mind-numbing work.

Using online tools, students can create roadmaps that show them the most direct path to a degree, steering them away from courses that don't count for their major, and helping them overcome common academic and financial obstacles. If students do badly in an introductory course that forecasts how they'll fare in more advanced classes, advisers can point out alternative disciplines where, the data indicate, they would be more likely to shine. And administrators can identify students who, from past experience with similar undergraduates, will benefit from extra help starting the day they're admitted.[17]

Those who champion big data anticipate a revolution in higher education. "This is going to be as big as computers," enthuses Ellen Wagner, who runs the Predictive Analytics Reporting Framework.[18]

When carefully used, big data carries outsized potential to enhance teaching and give students a better shot at graduating. But the 2018 Facebook-Cambridge Analytica mega-scandal stands as an ugly reminder of the potential abuses of data-mining. Of course higher education is not in the same mischief-making league, but there is also a dark side to the practice in academe.

Consider the events that unfolded, in 2016, at Mount St. Mary's College, in Maryland. Simon Newman, the new president, was desperate to improve the college's ranking. The former private-equity CEO came up with a novel way to raise graduation rates, which figure significantly in calculating those rankings—get rid of freshmen whose responses to a survey, administered when they arrived on campus, indicated that they might well leave school early. Professors were asked to identify weak students after the first few weeks of the semester. "My short-term goal is to have 20–25 people leave," Newman told the faculty. "This one thing will boost our retention 4–5 percent." Instead of educating the students the college had admitted, the president wanted to weed out those who could hurt its standing. There would be "collateral damage" to students who would have found their footing, he acknowledged, but that was a price worth paying. "This is hard for you because you think of the students as cuddly bunnies," Newman told balky professors, "but you can't. You just have to drown the bunnies . . . put a Glock to their heads."[19]

The Mount St. Mary's story is an extreme example of how data can lead to devilment if left in the wrong hands. But while most universities are less Machiavellian, they may well misuse the information they gather. "The stuff some colleges know right now about their students, thanks to the data-mining of their digital footprints, boggles the mind," Goldie Blumenstyk, a senior writer at *The Chronicle of Higher Education,* points out. "It may even seem a bit creepy."[20]

Administrators inattentive to concerns about students' privacy can crunch the numbers to extract detailed information about their out-of-classroom lives—whether they participate in online chatrooms; download lecture notes; frequent the library, the dining hall, or the health center; show up for the clubs they joined; or even buy a school hoodie—without the students being any the wiser.[21] A sharply worded email, informing students that "you're at risk," drafted by advisers who don't understand that algorithms don't spell destiny, can turn into a self-fulfilling prophesy, as students look for the exit sign. A data-based suggestion can become a diktat, when students whose performance in a course is less than stellar are told to "get real," to forget about their dream careers and settle for third best.

Data analytics can also confirm negative biases about poor and minority students, prompting institutions to stereotype all those who fit the statistical category by pushing them into unneeded mentoring and advising. What's far worse, the algorithm can be exploited to cement race and class prejudice.[22]

"Colleges will continue to use student and institutional data in new and innovative ways and will therefore have to occasionally reassess whether their ethical standards address current data practices," a 2016 New America report concludes.[23] How it's used is up to them—at least until a Cambridge Analytica-type scandal surfaces.

Making Undergraduates More Resilient

In the spring of 2003, ninety-two freshmen at a school that I'll call Elite U spent sixty minutes engaged in what must have felt like an innocuous exercise. Some were asked to read the results of what they were told was a survey of upperclassmen, together with ostensible firsthand reports of navigating college life. The stories detailed how, at first, these juniors and seniors felt snubbed by their classmates and intimidated by their professors, and how things turned around as they gained self-confidence. The freshmen wrote essays explaining how their own experiences dovetailed with those of the upperclassmen, and then videotaped talks, based on their essays, that would supposedly be shown to the next freshman class. Meanwhile, a control group was immersed in an unrelated topic.

This brief experience had no effect on the white students' academic performance, but it had a profound impact on the African American participants. By the time they graduated, their grades were a third of a point higher than their peers in the control group—that's the difference between B+ and A- average—and they had halved the black-white achievement gap. What's more, they reported being healthier and happier.[24]

Those of us who aren't psychologists are likely to be struck by the fact that so much can be accomplished in such a short period of time. Like magic spells cast by a modern-day Merlin, this sounds far too good to be true. Why should an hour-long experience carry so much punch? To the psychologists, however, what matters isn't the brevity but the believability of the experience. As David Yeager, at the University of Texas, and Greg Walton, at Stanford University, point out, in an article tellingly titled "Social-Psychological Interventions in Education: They're Not Magic," "even a seemingly small intervention but one that removes a critical barrier to learning can produce substantial effects on academic outcomes. They can be brief yet impactful because they target students' subjective experiences in school and because they rely on a rich tradition of research on persuasion and attitude change to powerfully convey psychological ideas."[25]

Some students, even those with gleaming high school records, believe that the college that admitted them made a mistake. Convinced that they aren't good enough to be there, they don't reach out to their classmates, who, they are certain, know more than they do, or to their professors, who, they are convinced, won't take them seriously. It's this attitude that the Elite U intervention was designed to target.

A related line of research, pursued by Carol Dweck, at Stanford, found that some students attributed their academic missteps to a lack of brain-power, unwittingly adopting the discredited theory that intelligence resides entirely in the genes. Dweck dubbed this a "fixed mindset," and she showed that those who embraced it fared poorly in school. Whether sweating a high school English paper or doing a college biochem experiment, if they didn't get the correct answer the first time, they assumed it was because they didn't have the intellectual horsepower. Frustrated, they gave up. But students with a "growth mindset"—the understanding that the brain, like any muscle, grows stronger with use—kept trying, rethinking their approach and seeking help if they remained stumped. As you'd anticipate, they fared much better.[26] Just as the Elite U experiment showed that a brief assignment could change students' views about whether they belonged in college, Dweck and her colleagues found that telling students how experience alters the architecture of the brain could lead them to adopt a growth mindset.

Both psychological strategies are designed to instill in students an awareness that they are masters of their own destiny, equipping them with tools to become more resilient when facing the foreseeable setbacks of college life. "Belonging" and "mindset" complement one another—if you think you aren't bright enough to do college-level work you're likely to regard yourself as an imposter.

Meanwhile, pathbreaking research by Claude Steele, at Stanford, found that—like Dweck's "fixed mindset" students, whom they resembled—minority undergraduates were especially prone to hold negative beliefs about their intelligence. Their antennae were sensitive to intimations that they were inherently less capable than their white classmates, and to take those slights to heart. In *Stigma,* a classic in sociology, Erving Goffman observed that "the central feature of the stigmatized individual's situation in life . . . is a question of . . . 'acceptance.'"[27] Steele labeled this tendency to doubt oneself as a "stereotype threat," and his research showed its disabling consequences. In one study, black undergraduates' test scores were considerably lower when they were told that the verbal GRE measured their intellectual ability than when the test was described as a problem-solving exam.[28]

The Elite U intervention was designed to challenge these destructive ways of thinking by showing that upperclassmen who had been in the same boat found ways to overcome their self-doubts. As the researchers suggested, "the intervention robbed adversity of its symbolic meaning for African Americans, untethering their sense of belonging from daily hardship."[29]

Freshman year marks the opportune moment to plant these concepts in the students' minds. It is at this pivot point, when students are leaving home and moving from the regimented world of high school to the laissez-faire university, that that they feel most at sea. This sense of insecurity makes them amenable to new ideas, especially when presented by an upper-classman. "Having someone who's a year or two older than you deliver this message makes an immense difference," Claude Steele points out. "The fundamental insight in the field is the power of narratives about ourselves and the circumstances we're in. The researchers are altering that narrative. What they've figured out is the value of relying on college students who've lived through the experience and come out the other side to deliver the message. That's a plausible voice—if I said the same thing, nobody would listen."

Alter an undergraduate's worldview, as happened to the Elite U students, and you set in motion a virtuous circle. The students who took to heart the idea of belonging found responsive classmates and helpful professors, and those initial breakthroughs made them even more willing to reach out. They were better equipped to cope with the *sturm und drang* of college, for they recognized that adversity was a transient phenomenon and not a life sentence.

"Because these psychological interventions are self-reinforcing, they can cause lasting improvements in motivation and achievement even when the original treatment message has faded," Greg Walton and David Yeager point out. "As students study and learn and build academic skills and knowledge, they are better prepared to learn and perform well in the future. As students feel more secure in their belonging in school and form better relationships with peers and teachers, these become sources of support that promote feelings of belonging and academic success later."

The reverberations of this altered sense of self persisted long after the Elite U students forgot how they had spent sixty minutes at the outset of their freshmen year. A follow-up investigation found that, in the initial stage of their careers, they were faring better professionally and personally. What spelled the difference was the social network they built while in college.[30]

As we'll see, these models have been successfully tested on a much larger scale at the University of Texas. But the researchers haven't exported them to other campuses. This is what you would expect, since most scholars focus on creating and publishing ideas, not marketing them. That's Dave Paunesku's mission. Paunesku earned his PhD at Stanford, studying with Greg Walton, and has coauthored several journal articles, but he isn't interested in a career in academe. In 2016, he founded PERTS, the Project for Education Research That Scales, to bridge the gap between research and practice by translating research findings into practical solutions for large numbers of new-gen students.

"For me, the driving force is about the impact, not the psychological theory," Paunesku tells me. "The potential to make a scalable impact is tremendous."

In the fall of 2017, the mindset and belonging activities went public. That year, fifty community colleges and regional universities, the types of institutions where the dropout problem is most acute, tried out these brief experiences on their freshmen.

Ivy Tech, an Indiana community college, had been beta-testing the mindset model since 2012. "Desperation was the motivation. Those of us in community colleges are really hungry for any strategy that will help students succeed," says Vice Chancellor Mary Ann Sellars. The growth mindset activity boosted the graduation and transfer rate by 20 percent, and skeptical faculty morphed into cheerleaders. "The generation we are mainly serving at the community college level responds to the growth mindset approach," economics professor Nancy McWilliams argues. "It encourages them, instead of cutting them off at the knees. It's a re-start button on self-motivation."

More than 100 colleges, twice as many as in the rollout year, signed up in 2018, and 100,000 freshmen participated in this online activity. "The next important question is whether we can get hundreds—thousands—of colleges to adopt these interventions in a way that ensures they remain effective," Dave Paunesku tells me. "If we're successful, we can measurably improve educational equity on an unprecedented scale and with unheard-of cost-effectiveness. It's enough to keep me motivated."

Rewriting the Curriculum

Data analytics and short psychological interventions are attractive to administrators because they don't intrude on the lives of deans and professors. The belonging or mindset experience is administered during orientation, before classes begin. Administrators design and manage the tools that extract valuable information about students from big data sets, and the information that's gleaned is used mainly by advisers, whose existence many professors barely acknowledge. Other common contrivances—assigning freshmen with similar interests to "learning communities" with a common course schedule, or constructing a summer course for freshmen who will gain from a jump-start on college—appeal to administrators because they are invisible elsewhere on the campus. They don't touch its beating heart, the classroom, where controversy resides.

But what's expedient isn't necessarily what's most effective. Spotting new students who are likely to have trouble in algebra, as data analytics can do, is a futile exercise unless the course becomes more student-friendly. Though a brief "mindset" experience may make undergraduates more resilient, it doesn't substitute for a well-taught electrical engineering class.

At Ivy Tech, a few professors were already embedding mindset principles into their courses when the college signed up with PERTS. "I try to implement different strategies even when I grade exams," Mary Ann Sellars says. "I write notes to students on every essay. One thing I try to do is talk about strengths, tell them they have that ability to succeed."

Sellars's approach to teaching comes straight from the growth mindset handbook, but at Ivy Tech she is the decided exception. "It's relatively easy to get the professors to accept these [short online] activities, but it's a lot harder to get them to incorporate mindset in how they manage their classes, to understand that it's not just a one-shot deal," acknowledges Ron Sloan, the former vice chancellor. Professors who take refuge in "maintaining standards" can stand in the way, adds Nancy McWillliams. "They believe 'I need to maintain rigor, I need to hold the line.' Students who have come from poverty, which in my opinion is trauma, don't respond to that kind of criticism." At Ivy Tech, as in other schools that are using the mindset activity, changing the way professors teach comes next. "We're still taking baby steps," says Sellars.

Enter the Carnegie Foundation for the Advancement of Teaching, a ten-minute drive from the Stanford campus. The courses developed at the Foundation are revolutionizing the field of remedial mathematics.

"The decision to focus on college math came out of a larger theory of how to improve education generally," Tony Bryk, president of the Foundation, observes. "The way we as an educational community have been trying to solve problems just hasn't been effective."

Bryk has been a trailblazer in the field of improvement science—start with a promising idea, test it with practitioners, evaluate the results, and keep tinkering. This mode of thinking has altered the face of healthcare, saving countless lives, and Bryk imported it to education.[31] "Tony's goal was to spread improvement science," says David Yeager, who signed on as a researcher at the Foundation when he was finishing his doctoral dissertation at Stanford. "He needed a context. He needed a thing that had a good base, but that after it worked initially, you could create a network to do continuous improvement."

Math was the logical focus because it's the biggest bugaboo for many undergraduates.[32] "Community college is the key gateway to opportunity and remedial math is the single biggest gatekeeper," Bryk points out. "Here was something we could improve. What we came up with would project up, to four-year schools, and down, to K–12." In University of Texas professor Uri Treisman, Tony Bryk found the right collaborator, a mathematician whose research on undergraduates' math phobia had earned him national renown.

The curriculum-writers at the Foundation set out to design a course that would accomplish the seemingly impossible—to bring students who stumbled over fractions through college-level statistics in a single year. The course, called Statway, is built on three core principles. The first concerns the content of the course: students need to know why the topics they are studying will be useful to them. The second has to do with how the material is presented: the students are expected to reason their way to an answer rather than simply memorizing the correct response. Third, and hardest, the students' fear of math must be overcome.[33]

"I was reading the research that was coming out of Stanford," says Bryk, who had previously taught there. "It was hard to believe that short-term interventions could change long-term outcomes." But after a year of pursuing dead-end approaches, he wanted to hear from the social psychologists.

"These students have years of scar tissue around math," observes Yeager. "Every day, they don't want to belong there. In their minds, the fact that they are there means that they screwed up. That is a very scary place for people to be. The question was 'how do you complement the curricular reform with some psychology that allows people to feel safe?'" Yeager watched hours of videotaped focus group sessions conducted before, during and after students took remedial math. It was a sobering experience. "Those students entered with high hopes, but by the third week the life had been drained from their faces."

The Stanford researchers who designed the mindset and belonging experiences jumped at the opportunity to embed these habits of mind into the content of a college course. "Psychological interventions can work hand in hand with other reforms, such as those aimed at curriculum or pedagogy," they pointed out, in a report on "tenacity."[34] Although the brief activities were helpful to minority students, the researchers were adamant that they didn't let universities off the hook. As Greg Walton says, "It's the engine oil, not the engine."

"I've been pushing the social psychologists to think of the ethics of one-shot interventions," Uri Treisman tells me. "The question is, how do you create an environment where belonging, capability, purpose, mindsets, concerns about autonomy are all present, an environment in which the right supports for improved learning take root and allow students the freedom to learn?"

The psychologists crafted a mindset- and belonging-focused approach to math, devising a set of exercises for the first three weeks of class. At that point, explains Yeager, "if you're saying, 'I'm no good at this, I don't belong,' then you are gone. We tried to make a decline in confidence feel like a normal part of college. Then, when you raise the intellectual standards, make the work more rigorous, and deal with students' histories, students are willing to engage with this kind of deeper work."

The community college instructors on the course development team were dubious, for these activities were leagues away from their teaching experience. To address their concerns, the Foundation conducted a matched-sample experiment, with half the students in a math class participating in a thirty-minute growth mindset experience. When these students' grades improved, the model was tested on a larger group. The effects were equally positive, and those results brought the math teachers on board.

Improvement science pivots on evaluation, and it was no contest when Statway was pitted against a conventional remedial course. Only 5 percent of the remedial math students earned college-level math credit in one year, and even with an extra year of class just 15 percent reached that goal. Almost four times as many Statway students passed college math in a single year. What matters even more, half of them transferred to a four-year institution.[35] These findings have prompted a growing number of schools to adopt the course, and the University of Washington system has accepted Statway as meeting the math requirement.

Still, the going has been slow as the old ways die hard—in 2016–2017, just 7,522 students enrolled in Statway. As we'll see, CUNY's community colleges are among those that adapted the course while maintaining its underlying principles, and this kind of reworking is all to the good. But college math departments elsewhere have resisted. The California State University system, which enrolls nearly half a million students, flirted with the curriculum, but ultimately said no. "About half of their students need remediation," Karon Klipple, director of the Carnegie Math Pathways, tells me. "The math chairs felt that all students, regardless of their career trajectories, need intermediate algebra. They didn't see the value in quantitative reasoning and critical thinking skills that Statway teaches." Other colleges that have tried using Statway abandoned it after a year or two, concluding that it was too hard to teach.

"Colleges want the magic worksheet," Yeager observes resignedly. "Then people will do unthoughtful replications and say, 'see, your magic worksheet doesn't work, you guys were liars all along.' "[36]

I asked Geoff Cohen where his and his Stanford colleagues' theories came from. "We took them from good teachers," he replied. On every campus, you'll find professors committed to doing better by their students, and while they may not be familiar with the social psychologists' findings, their redesigned courses often incorporate the same principles—the material is calculated to evoke students' interest, the teaching is more student-centered and the professors make a point of being attentive to their students' insecurities. We will meet several of these professors at Long Beach State. But a handful of faculty members, siloed within their own departments, do not represent a movement.

The situation would improve a lot quicker if university leaders made teaching a major factor in promotion and tenure decisions, but that's rarely the case. "I was warned that getting involved with the curriculum was a sure way for me to lose my job," Bill Powers, the former president of the University of Texas, recalls. As we'll see, he persevered, and the university is better off for it, but there aren't many campus leaders as gutsy as he.

So, too, with Statway. "You need a president or provost to shine a light on the problem, and say, 'This is how bad the current situation is. It's unacceptable and we need an evidence-based solution to change it,'" says Karon Klipple. "But that rarely happens."

Mark Becker, president of Georgia State University, was even blunter when I asked him why so many schools were blind to the remedial math morass. "Colleges keep looking for the easy way out. Rewriting the curriculum is hard."

CONNECTING THE DOTS

The community college student sounded disconsolate, and devoid of hope. "I'm tired of school," he told an interviewer. "I had a plan and thought I was doing everything right, and everyone I talked to seemed so sure they were giving me the right information, so I never questioned it because I had no idea what I was doing. But here I am and I've probably lost two whole semesters taking classes I didn't need or that ended up not transferring or counting toward my major. I don't even want to think about the money I lost, because I couldn't afford to lose it. At this point, honestly, I don't know if I'm ever going to finish. I'm just getting tired."

Each autumn, about 40 percent of all first-time college students enroll in community colleges. While they may not have fared well in high school, the promise of success—an associate degree, transfer to a university, a bachelor's degree—dangles like the elusive rabbit in a greyhound race. More than 80 percent of them say that earning a BA is their goal.[37]

Those who transfer to a four-year institution have a better chance of graduating than their classmates who came straight from high school.[38] But enrolling in a university can seem like an insurmountable challenge for a community college student. As the dispirited student's story illustrates, overcoming the institutional barriers is a formidable task.[39]

These students often lack confidence in their ability, and they're prone to blame themselves when things go wrong, but the biggest culprit is the transfer process itself. Overburdened and ill-informed community college advisers tell them to take courses that a university won't accept. Half of community college transfers lose a significant amount of their course credit, which costs them time and money.[40] "I'd rather look for myself than ask for somebody to answer the questions, because I've had cases where those questions weren't answered correctly, and since they're not answered correctly it's a big, big mistake," another community college student lamented.

Even if a transfer student receives credit for a class, the university may refuse to count it toward a major. You can hear the professors' refrain—"our Chem 1 class is more rigorous"—and in that circumstance the student must repeat the course. A community college may come to an agreement about admission or course credit with one campus of a state university, but the terms of this treaty aren't acceptable to the faculty at another campus in the same system.[41] As Jack Scott, the former chancellor of California's community college system, ruefully observes, community college and university faculty alike "tend to make decisions more in an academic atmosphere rather than in the interest of students."[42]

These problems can be overcome when universities and community colleges combine forces to devise a glide-path leading straight from one school to the other. [43]

If collaboration across campuses is going to work, faculty on both sides of the institutional divide need to set aside their preconceptions—community college professors' belief they care more about teaching, and university professors' conviction that community college gives its students a watered-down education. As we'll see, Valencia College and the University of Central Florida, its Orlando neighbor, are among the institutions that have pulled this off. Since 2003, every Valencia graduate has been guaranteed admission to UCF. The guarantee gives community college students an extra incentive to earn their associate degree, and since the agreement was adopted Valencia's graduation rate has nearly doubled.

These strategies are all well known to most university leaders. But knowing is one thing, and acting on that knowledge is a very different matter. As we'll see in the following campus accounts, it's essential that higher education leaders put student success atop their to-do list. They have to be sufficiently adroit to persuade the campus constituencies that there's a serious problem—and one that can be fixed. What's more, they need the managerial know-how to convert big ideas into on-the-ground change. That's the case at each school we will be visiting.

2

GEORGIA STATE UNIVERSITY
High Tech, High Touch

Half a century ago, Georgia State University was an open admissions institution—but open only to whites. Fifteen years ago, the institution, a cluster of characterless buildings a few blocks from downtown Atlanta, was a big, poor-performing commuter school that, like its counterparts elsewhere, had low graduation rates and yawningly wide racial gaps. Fewer than one in three students graduated. Minority students did even worse—only 29 percent of African Americans and 22 percent of Latinos earned bachelor's degrees.

The faculty attributed those sorry results to the undergraduates' underwhelming high school education. "How can we be a national model when I have students who can't write?" lamented one member of the old guard.

How things have changed—since 2003, the graduation rate has climbed to 54 percent, considerably higher than comparable schools. Among nonprofit universities, it ranks first, nationwide, in the number of African American graduates.[1] What's especially impressive is that *minority, first-generation, and low-income students are earning degrees at a higher rate than their white classmates.*

Georgia State didn't tackle its dropout crisis by recruiting better-pedigreed students, as some universities have done. On the contrary—in recent years, the undergraduates have become poorer and more racially diverse, and the average SAT score has declined by thirty-three points. Three out of five students are black and Latino. A similar number are eligible for federal Pell Grants, earmarked for needy students. "The school enrolls more students on Pell Grants than any other public research university, and more than the entire eight-university Ivy League—by a nearly 3-to-1 margin."[2]

The university has forged a strategy that works for the students it has. Tim Renick, the paladin for graduation rates (formally, Vice President for Enrollment Management and Student Success), brings the passion of a preacher to his position. "Despite the conventional wisdom, demographics are not destiny," he tells me. "Rather than blaming the students, we took a hard look in the mirror."

For Renick, and many of those I spoke with when I visited the campus, this is a bedrock moral issue. "As long as we assume that these students are destined to graduate at lower rates, we are just replicating a system that is based on inequality and injustice."

It's hard to exaggerate the magnitude—and the national implications—of what Georgia State University has accomplished:

*It was the first university to build a data analytics system that's linked to one-on-one advising.

*It was the first university to use nudges as a way to ensure that admitted students make it to campus.

*It embedded the importance of "growth mindset" and "social belonging" in the lives of freshmen, relying on a cadre of peer mentors and counselors.

*It rewrote the freshman math curriculum, substituting hands-on courses for big lectures, and is headed in the same direction with big introductory classes.

*It was the first university to give just-in-time small grants to juniors and seniors who had been dropping out because they were a few hundred dollars short.

*Together with Arizona State, it launched the University Innovation Alliance, which shares promising practices with ten other big public universities.

By dramatically boosting its graduation rate and wiping out its achievement gap, Georgia State has demolished the farrago of excuses that colleges have generated to rationalize their abysmal track record. Administrators regularly make the trek to Atlanta—more than a hundred of them every year, by Renick's count, as if the university were Lourdes—but those who hope for a quick and easy fix are doomed to disappointment.

The good news regarding the dropout scandal is that we know what must be done to end it. But it is tough sledding for any campus leader to make student success, rather than institutional prestige, as defined by its place on the *U.S. News* pecking order, the top priority. To accomplish this requires the courage to confront deeply held conventional wisdoms, something that few college presidents have demonstrated.

MANY LITTLE THINGS

The crucial first step in rewriting Georgia State's script of failure was to figure out why so many students were leaving. "We had hundreds of students dropping out every semester without a word," Tim Renick told me. "They never spoke to an adviser, came to tutoring, discussed their plans. They were just gone."

The effort to address this problem began in earnest in 2010, with a close-grained analysis of a decade's worth of students' grades, 2.5 million in all, to specify the factors that affected a student's chances of getting a degree. Scrutinizing the data enabled Tim Renick and his colleagues to hone in on the biggest obstacles to student success. The next step was figuring out how to overcome them.

Data was the driver. The university has been the nation's leader in using predictive analytics to inform its decisions about everything from determining which freshmen should get a head start by coming to campus the summer before classes start to figuring out which upperclassmen, on the verge of dropping out, need a small, just-in-time grant to graduate.

Data doesn't tell you anything—it's just a jumble of numbers—but pose the right questions and you can glean valuable insights from dissecting masses of information. For instance, when universities track students' academic progress, they typically consider whether they pass or fail a course, not their actual grade. But Georgia State learned that the grade itself makes a big difference—there, a student who earns a B in, say, first-year political science has a 70 percent chance of graduating in that field, while a classmate who gets a C has only a 25 percent chance. Now the student who receives a C talks with an adviser, getting a dollop of tutoring before that grade turns into a D or F in more advanced courses. "When we began to let students know they were at academic risk and offer help we began to see the graduation gaps go away," says Renick.

Here's another example. The nursing faculty assumed that the anatomy and physiology class was the best indicator of how a student would fare in the major, and so, in determining whom to admit to this highly selective field, it relied on the grade in that course. But when those professors were informed that algebra and chemistry were in fact better predictors, the department altered its admission criteria. Instead of having to wait until junior year to find out whether they can study nursing, students now have a pretty clear answer by the end of their freshman year, which gives them ample time to explore other options.

The data also showed that new-gen students are reluctant to seek help from their professors, so the university hired upperclassmen as tutors. A third of Georgia State undergraduates are being tutored, and those who go to at least three sessions do half a letter-grade better (a B versus a B-), and are 10 percent likelier to graduate. "The material is exactly what the teacher went over," film major Ellie Thompson tells me, "but because it's a peer it's more relatable."

The biggest pitfalls, at Georgia State and big public universities generally, are the required college math classes. In 2009, nearly half of the students got Ds and Fs in those courses. Not only did they have to retake the class, sometimes more than once, they also lost the state scholarships that kept them financially afloat. After these courses were converted from the classic lecture format to a class in which they spend most of their time in a computer lab, with immediate online feedback and instructors at the ready, the number of Ds and Fs plummeted to 19 percent. As I saw when I visited the lab, this is an infinitely livelier way to learn—instead of half paying attention as the professor marches through a PowerPoint presentation, students beaver away on computers, proceeding at their own pace, while tutors roam the room to field questions.

The revamping of the math courses was mandated by the campus administration, and it encountered considerable resistance. "We're trying to charm people into changing behavior," says Renick, and the new curriculum was given a thorough road-test before being widely implemented. "The outcomes weren't just a little better, but a lot better, and consistently so—not just for minority students but for all students." If charm and data don't do the trick, blunter methods are used—the math department chair who insisted that the onus for students' failing grades was on the public schools lost his position.

When predictive analytics was introduced, faculty skeptics anticipated that students would be pushed into easier fields, with would-be scientists steered into sociology. In fact, it's exactly the opposite—computer science and biology are the fastest-growing majors, and twice as many black students are graduating with science-related degrees. Sink or swim used to be how the university handled students who wanted to be STEM majors, despite having had limited exposure to math and science in high school. Now these students get help even before their first semester. Standards haven't been lowered—pre-med students still take organic chemistry—but Georgia State is offering underprepared students what they need in order to make it.

Some professors feared that relying on big data would result in a power grab by the administration, but after seeing the positive impact of data analytics many of them caught the data bug. "When we changed the critical thinking class, the biggest in the university, from a flat-out lecture into a flipped class—watch lectures outside class on video, do group projects in class—we got a 17 percent increase in students' grades," George Rainbolt, the former chair of the philosophy department, tells me. "We had to try a ton of stuff and look at the data to see which interventions worked and which didn't."

"I'm interested in justice and equal educational opportunity," Rainbolt responds, when I ask him why a political philosopher became curious about data-mining. "There is a notion of philosophy as removed from the world, but I want to know what is just in the current world."

Many little things, not one big thing, explain Georgia State's track record—this isn't sexy stuff, but it works. "The currency of this strategy is the seemingly small win," according to a 2016 Boston Consulting Group report commissioned by the university. "No barrier is too small to address, and priority is determined by tractability as much as by scope or prominence. By accumulating many of these small wins—a few hundred students helped here, a few hundred there—the aggregate impact swells. The interventions are designed not to prove a theory but to attack a barrier."

Making Student Success Priority #1

Every university president faces a jam-packed agenda—raise money, build classrooms and dorms, massage faculty egos, coddle alumni, respond to crises, negotiate with state lawmakers. Doing something to stanch the flow of dropouts requires a leader like Georgia State president Mark Becker, someone who's fixated on student success and willing to break a few eggs if that's what it takes.

At precisely 9 AM every Wednesday morning, in the boardroom of Centennial Hall, Becker meets with his top administrators. In the corridor, banners herald the university's academic accomplishments—the law school ranks seventeenth among public law schools, ahead of better-known institutions like UC Davis and the University of Washington, and it's twelfth-best in computer science. The president is all business—black suit, starched white shirt, and blue tie—and everyone else is similarly attired. There's no doubt who's the boss. "Decision-making has become more centralized, and Mark has certainly made some enemies," business school dean Rich Phillips confides. "But he needed to make some enemies—it's part and parcel of leadership."

The importance of student success framed the presentation of each topic on the agenda at the session I sat in on. When he introduced the new football coach, Shawn Elliott, Becker made a point of mentioning that the university's "student success work is very important to the families of incoming athletes." When the discussion turned to recruiting faculty, he stressed "how important it is to diversify the professoriate. We have to be one of the institutions that steps up and does this. This is very personal—we *have* to do this." The administrators burst into applause after Tim Renick distributed a report from Education Trust that lauded Georgia State for eliminating the graduation gap for African American students.

"I was a military brat," Becker tells me. "You get resilience from being a military kid—you get used to change." His parents, who never went beyond high school, were adamant that their three sons go to college, but he was the "trouble-child, impatient. I wanted to join the military and jump out of planes." His parents were having none of it, and when a Marine Corps recruiter came to his home, they asked him to leave. He enrolled at the local community college, then moved on to Towson University and later to Penn State, where he got his PhD. He was intellectually restless, his focus shifting from engineering to physics to math. "I fell in love with the process of discovery, and I wanted to make a difference. I had a calling that took me away from pure math," he says, and that commitment led him to specialize in biostatistics and healthcare. He progressed swiftly in academe, as a professor at the University of Florida and then at the University of Michigan.

Though Becker never imagined himself as an administrator—"I had never even attended a faculty senate meeting"—an Ann Arbor colleague convinced him that he could have an outsized impact in that role. "I was outspoken, sometimes a minority voice," he recalls, describing himself as having been right often enough to be chosen as dean of the University of Minnesota public health school; there, he pushed the institution toward paying greater attention to the region's health needs.

Becker became the president of Georgia State in 2010, at the height of the Great Recession. "Never let a good crisis go to waste—when money is tight, you can do hard things, you can trim the fat," he tells me, putting a hoary managerial maxim to good use. He laid off 150 staff, because "there were too many assistant deans and administrators." By not cutting a single faculty position he endeared himself to the faculty, whom he was counting on to accept the changes that were coming.

New presidents are expected to produce a new strategic plan. Becker was dubious—"those plans usually sit on a shelf"—and so he took a distinctive approach. Keep it simple, he told the committee charged with crafting the document. Faculty and students would have a chance to comment on the draft and local residents could voice their opinions at town-hall-style meetings. "If you're going to legislators and planning a capital campaign, you should figure out how the plan will resonate in the community."

"Improving graduation rates" was the third priority in the draft plan. Becker moved it to the top. "If we're going to do it, we have to go big. Let's put ourselves out there and establish a national model."

Student applications were down at the time because of the economic climate. The provost wanted to cut the size of the freshmen class, raising the minimum SAT score required for admission, in order to move up the *US News* rankings. But this didn't sit well with Becker. "Will students with low SAT scores graduate?" he asked Renick, who assured him they would. That was good enough for Becker. "We're never going to break the top fifty in the rankings. Instead of trying to compete with the University of Georgia, let's graduate who we enroll."

The admissions criteria were redesigned: rather than stressing scores on the SAT test—on which minority students, acutely aware of the pressure to prove themselves, often do badly—added weight is given to high school grades, which do a better job of forecasting how students will fare.[3] In essence, any high school student with a B average now gets admitted.

That decision has cost the university dearly in the *U.S. News* rankings. "You get bonus points for turning down very qualified students," says Renick. "We've made a moral commitment to do the opposite." State politicians keep pressing Becker to make the school look stronger on paper by becoming more selective, but their arguments go nowhere with him. "I just had a meeting with the chancellor [of the university system] and the governor. There are still some attitudes about getting better students. What I say is that our admissions standards are the line and if you meet the standard you can come here." He makes a dollar-and-cents argument for the model: "Our graduates earn $72,000 after ten years, not the $23,000 their parents are earning."

Moving the needle on the number of graduates demands not only a tough-minded president, like Mark Becker, but also a second-in-command with the skills and dedication to put those commitments into on-the-ground realities. That's Tim Renick's job. Most universities split responsibility for what's called "student support" among a host of units—admissions, counseling, advising, financial aid, and the like, with each unit going its own way. Students' legitimate concerns vanish amid the bureaucratic jockeying. Renick's portfolio encompasses everything that affects students' lives outside the classroom, from admissions to career placement.

Tim Renick's style is more relaxed than Mark Becker's, and that difference is palpable in the weekly session of his top staffers. There was lots of banter during the meeting I attended; ties were loosened and jackets shed. But despite the casualness, this is indisputably Tim Renick's show.

The agenda invariably focuses on hard-core data. Those who work with college students characteristically see the world through the prism of the personal, but here it is the wonks who rule.

The conversation at this meeting centered on a newly adopted strategy to get more newly admitted freshmen to enroll.[4] In the past, nearly a fifth of students who were accepted and paid their registration fees never showed up. "Summer melt," the phenomenon is called, and Georgia State was the first university to field-test a new, light-touch approach to combatting it— a text-messaging "nudge" campaign, designed by University of Pittsburgh economist Lindsay Page, with reminders sent to students who needed to fill out federal financial aid forms, sign up for orientation or choose their classes.

The campaign had been a roaring success, the admissions director reported. The number of no-shows was reduced by 20 percent, and although the same number of students had been admitted the previous year, the new freshman class had 350 more students.

On most campuses that make use of data analytics, a self-described "data geek" in a senior role invariably takes the initiative.[5] Ethicists aren't usually data geeks, but this is the path Tim Renick has chosen. "My ethics commitment pulled me into this position," he tells me, when I ask him how a religion professor became the number-crunching good shepherd for Georgia State undergraduates.

Tim Renick's father, like Mark Becker's, was in the military, but there the similarities end. While Becker was the rebel, Renick was perennially the by-the-books student. Growing up on Long Island, he was an outsider twice over, poor and gentile in a wealthy, predominantly Jewish community. "We lived in the poorest part of town. My best friend lived in the house where the swimming pool party orgy in 'Great Gatsby' was filmed." Renick was valedictorian of his high school class; went to Dartmouth, where he ranked sixth in his class ("I was clueless about an elite institution," he recalls); and earned a PhD in religion from Princeton in four years.

Hired by Georgia State at age twenty-five and tasked with starting a religious studies department, Renick immediately plunged into administration. He chaired search committees, pitched the regents for funds, and ran the honors college. "I always loved statistics," he says, recalling the hundreds of hours he spent playing a virtual baseball game called Strat-o-Matic when he was in elementary school. That love served him well at the university. "When I was chair of religious studies, I argued to the dean that, although we were small, we were high-impact. Not only were we teaching a lot of students, our graduates were going to the top PhD programs in the country."

Right person, right job—Tim Renick personifies Georgia State's marriage of dedication and information, ethics, and numbers. He embodies what the Boston Consulting Group report describes as "a culture of data-driven decision-making, experimentation and accountability."

ONE-TO-ONE CONNECTIONS

Georgia State has received lots of praise, and deservedly so, for its pioneering use of big data. But while college administrators elsewhere rush to mine their cache of information, as if this were the answer to their prayers, Tim Renick knows that number-crunching, without more, isn't nearly enough. An electronic "adviser," which cash-strapped universities have been turning to as a substitute for flesh-and-blood advisers, can show students the surest path to graduation. But a computer program cannot help them think through whether it is the direction they want to take—for that, they need to speak with a knowledgeable professional. Renick is convinced that what best explains the accomplishments of Georgia State's students are these personal connections, which reach from admission to graduation.

Rhetoric about student success is boilerplate-easy, but a university's budget shows where its priorities lie, and Georgia State has made a major investment in advising. Even as the university suffered a big hit during the Great Recession, Mark Becker hired a raft of advisers. Now there's one for every 300 students, down from one for every 1,500. While elite colleges can afford to have many more professionals on the ground, this ratio is far better than you'll find at similar institutions. Students can pick up signals, and the import of locating the advising center in prime campus real estate hasn't been lost on them.

"From medieval times, the mentoring relationship was the key, and that's still true," Tim Renick points out. "Look at how top colleges keep student-faculty ratios low so that students get more attention. Most big public universities haven't tried to deliver this kind of attention, and when budgets were cut, advisers were the first to go. We've used technology to identify who needs personalized attention, so we can deliver it at scale. 'Your problems are our problems; you are valued'—that's the message. If students don't feel that, then they leave."

There are more than 50,000 advising sessions at Georgia State every year. I was a fly on the wall at one of them.

Sydney Brayn looked nervous when she walked into room 007A, adviser Emily Buis's office. Sydney had transferred to Georgia State from Savannah State, a historically black school, the year before. She planned to major in journalism, but that wasn't working out, for Sydney was scraping by with Cs, and journalism students must maintain a B average. This meeting, Sydney's fifth with an adviser in the span of a semester and a half, would chart her academic future.

"Why did you want to study journalism?" Emily asks Sydney at the start of the meeting. "I have a fascination with celebrities, and I wanted to interview them," she replied. "Then I decided to change to media studies because I want to be behind the scenes, writing and editing."

"This shift is really a blessing in disguise," Emily tells her. "It sounds like the media is your real interest, and the department is expanding because the film industry is coming to Atlanta. You'll develop the technical skills, like learning to use a camera, and that's a great experience. The writing can come later." And if Sydney didn't meet the media studies requirements, a film major remained an option. "Here are all the things you can do with that major," Emily says, showing her a host of media jobs on the university's website.

To deliver the soundest advice, Emily had to understand why Sydney was doing so badly, and the discussion segued to Sydney's personal life. Like most students at Georgia State, she has to work. The Kroger grocery store, where she was a cashier, decided what hours she worked on a week-to-week basis, and that made it hard to get to her classes. What's more, she was living at home, an hour-and-a-half commute to campus. "Spring vacation is coming up," Emily reminds her. "It's a good time to look for a better job, and there are opportunities to live in campus housing."

Emily already knew a lot about Sydney before the session—not only her grades but also the myriad factors that, the data show, made her a risky bet for graduation. If things are going awry, what's the problem—grades? attendance? acting out in class? But while this information informs how Emily thinks, she doesn't focus on the numbers but on the student sitting across her desk.

Some undergraduates steer clear of their adviser, hoping they can wish the problem away, but Georgia State doesn't wait until they are on the knife-edge of failing. To seize their attention, it places a hold on their accounts, which prevents them from registering for classes. "You're required to see your adviser," says pre-law major Anna Pak, "and they've really helped me because they act like a friend would act. They understand what we going through, they get the drama about money. You can tell them the truth."

As Joshua Walker, another adviser, tells me, "I'm like a smart friend. Students say 'I don't know how' and I get them back on track." Unlike their counterparts at other universities, whose duties are confined to academics, these advisers are also responsible for making sure students receive the maximum financial aid to which they're entitled, often helping them fill out the complicated FAFSA (Free Application for Federal Student Aid) form. Money, academics, life outside of school—it's one-stop shopping for students.

"You're in a puddle, but you can jump out of that puddle," Emily reassures Sydney. "We'll make it work—that's what we're here for."

"It's not like Savannah State, where nobody helped you," Sydney tells me after the session. She is a bit overwhelmed but excited about her future. "Here they have a high regard for individual students. My parents told me I was going to college or the military, and I thought college could help me find out who I can be. My three brothers and sisters dropped out of community college, and now I'm this close to getting a degree."

When I wrote about Georgia State, in a *New York Times* column, I received a slew of emails from readers who blasted the university's approach to advising as coddling students, instead of letting them learn from their own mistakes—the "helicopter university" substituting for helicopter parents. "When I went to college I had to make it on my own" went the typical message.

These "I walked five miles, uphill, to and from school every day" pontificators don't understand how different their lives were, how much they gained from having a raft of support. They don't take into account the hard-knocks lives led by many students at schools like Georgia State—an at-best mediocre high school education, no one at hand who knows the ropes, money a constant source of angst.

Startlingly, it is estimated that half of all college students struggle with food insecurity and one undergraduate in ten has no place to call their own.[6] Data-plus-advising cannot solve these problems—"we just don't have the money to meet those needs," Mark Becker laments—but it helps to level the scholastic playing field.

Changes That Work

Experiment, test, expand—every step Georgia State has taken to improve the lives of students harnesses data at the service of the personal.

With more than 30,000 undergraduates, the university can be a daunting place, whether for a white student from rural Georgia who has never ventured to Atlanta or a poor African American student from Atlanta who has rarely gone downtown. To combat this feeling of isolation, freshmen with similar academic interests are split into small groups, enclaves of intimacy called learning communities, and they take a common suite of classes. While many schools have adopted the learning communities model, Georgia State has taken it a crucial step further—each cadre collaborates on a project, like building houses with Habitat for Humanity, to instill what Renick describes as "a sense of place and belonging."[7]

Undergraduate tutors, embedded in over a thousand courses, are trained in the tools of belonging and growth mindset. "The theory behind having fellow undergraduates in this role," Renick adds, "is to show that 'someone like me can master even the toughest material.'"

"They thought I was dumb." That's how Kayla Patterson, a pre-nursing student, reacted when her acceptance letter came with a caveat—she had to enroll in the university's Summer Success Academy. Its chirpy name didn't fool her, "but I came to appreciate it." Although the Academy is tailored for newly minted freshmen who, on the basis of their test scores and high school records, are at greatest risk of not making it, this isn't a four-week summer session for dummies. In addition to a "how-to-succeed-in-college" course that teaches survival skills like time management, they take introductory social science classes side by side with upperclassmen.

"It's not just four weeks of the weakest students," says Renick. "We know the power of providing examples. We're exposing students to peers who look like them and have figured out how to 'do college,' so that they can see the norm." These freshmen are also assigned undergraduate mentors, many of whom went through the program a year or two earlier. The model has proven itself—90 percent complete their freshman year, a better track record than their classmates.

"The more I participated, the more I learned about myself and what I'm capable of achieving," says TaNia Vaughn, a freshman who wants to become a nurse. "I have to show them I'm capable of achieving whatever I set out to do. After doing all these programs and activities, I had a leg up because people who came in in the fall didn't know about the resources. It hit me after the first test in philosophy, when I realized college and high school are two different things. In high school, I could sleep in class, study the night before and do fine, but in college that's not the case. I didn't do badly on my first test, but I could have been more prepared, and I could tell. The transition was in learning how to prioritize and set aside times to study and manage my time. And the people I met my first week there are still my best friends. I've applied to be a mentor—I want to give something back."

The mentors are trained in helping their charges see the benefits of maintaining a don't-give-up, growth-oriented view of yourself, and this attitude resonated with pre-med student Cabria de Chabert. "My mentor is my role model. She does so much—how does she do it? It's a matter of your mindset and how badly you want something, mind over matter. You control the things around you." Initially fearful about approaching her professors, Cabria got "tips about not psyching myself out about the possible scenarios and what's going to happen, so I learned to go into a meeting with a positive mindset and let things unfold. One time I went to the professor and talked to him, and I got an A. Before I went there I thought that I was going to fail."

Why did more than a thousand seniors who were only a handful of credits shy of graduating drop out every year? That's what Tim Becker wanted to know. These students' behavior seemed irrational—they were leaving the university saddled with debt but without a diploma.

A green-eyeshade review revealed that, in many instances, their financial aid had run out and they were short less than $1,000. What's true at Georgia State is the case nationwide—research shows that, regardless of their grades, students are more likely to drop out if they lose even small amounts of assistance.[8]

In 2012, the university became the first in the country to make no-strings awards to these students to keep them in school. "We'd call the students to tell them we were giving them $500 or $1,000 and at first they thought it was a scam," Tim Renick remembers. The approach has proven itself. In 2017, nearly two thousand juniors and seniors returned to the classroom, and two semesters after receiving a grant, almost all of them had graduated or were on their way to earning a degree.

To look at Kalif Robinson's academic record—a straight-A average, an international affairs honors student minoring in Arabic, and training to be a diplomat—you'd never know that, frantic about paying for school while also helping to support his parents, he was on the verge of what he describes as a nervous breakdown. "I had a great mentor and friend at the Study Abroad office. She was receptive and 'organic' with me, and when she told me about the grant it literally changed my life."

Kalif wants to contribute something in return, "making myself a resource to other students." Previous surveys of graduating seniors had shown that many students denigrated the university as a tuition-hungry bureaucracy, but the just-in-time grants prompted them to appreciate that it was on their side. Research confirms that "both the dollars and the psychological impact of the support from the institution in a time of crisis are likely to make a difference."[9]

TACKLING THE BIG-TICKET COURSES

Ask most university leaders what they're doing to help students graduate and they'll point you to scores of initiatives. But few of these undertakings reach more than a handful of students and none of those programs has likely been evaluated. Here as elsewhere, Georgia State does things differently— try out a promising idea, evaluate whether it works, then junk it or adopt it campus-wide.

The university learned that freshmen are likelier to return for their sophomore year when they attend college-credit courses while simultaneously receiving out-of-class tutoring, rather than being consigned to dead-end remedial education. The same holds true for freshmen who belong to a learning community, as well as those who take foundation classes in a broad field, like STEM or education, before settling on a specific major, like computer science or counseling. When initiatives like these prove their worth, they go universal.

As they noodled about how to cut the dropout rate, Becker and Renick dug into almost every aspect of campus life. But there was a conspicuous exception—apart from freshman math, no attention had been paid to instruction. As Renick points out, "many of the changes we have made at Georgia State do not disrupt the faculty. Advising, nudges, mini-grants, and learning communities don't ask the faculty to do anything differently." Though this laissez-faire approach sounds odd—after all, teaching and learning form the core of a university's mission—these administrators were acting prudently. Professors vehemently resist top-down attempts to alter what should be taught or how to teach it.[10]

"You can't start with the faculty because that will end unhappily," Renick acknowledges. But the university's graduation rate had remained stagnant for several years running, leading the top administrators to conclude that they had squeezed all the juice from the outside-the-classroom innovations. If more students were going to earn bachelor's degrees, the classroom door had to be prized open.

At Georgia State, the ten most popular introductory courses enroll thirty thousand undergraduates each semester, five thousand in the American government class alone. Students who received at least a B in these classes were likely to earn a bachelor's degree, but upward of 15 percent got Ds and Fs, or else they withdrew. To have a hope of earning a degree, they had to take the course a second time, and things spiraled downhill from there. Change those outcomes and many more students would stay in school—that was the lesson from the revamping of freshman math.

These super-size introductory courses rely almost entirely on lectures. But if students do most of the learn-the-content work on their own, with online exercises to test whether they understand the material, then classtime can be used for think-work. Altering the pedagogy radically affects outcomes—research shows that students in these hands-on classes are half as likely to flunk as those in lecture classes.[11]

In characteristic data-driven fashion, the university is conducting an experiment that pits the old pedagogy against the new, to determine whether more students in these redesigned courses earn passing grades and whether they do better in advanced courses.

If this flipped classroom model works best, as seems likely, it's the way every faculty member will be expected to teach. It's no easy task for professors who have lectured for their entire career to make this switch, but Renick thinks the evidence will be the convincer. "There are not many things that link faculty members in English and Accounting, but they all have been trained in research and appreciate the data."

SPREAD THE WORD—THE UNIVERSITY INNOVATION ALLIANCE

Universities habitually compete with one another on a host of fronts, including how well they do in the *U.S. News* beauty contest and the dollars they rake in. They poach professors and lure top students from one another, and their rivalries, on and off the field, are the stuff of legend.

Several years ago at an Aspen Institute conference, Mark Becker and Michael Crow, president of Arizona State, another wellspring of innovation, huddled over how their two schools might do things differently, swapping ideas about how to improve graduation rates and expand opportunities for new-gen students.

"The Next Generation University," a New America Foundation report, catalyzed the conversation. "The need to give more students access to high-quality public universities is clear. Yet many public colleges and universities are failing to respond," the report concluded, while praising the two universities for "expanding enrollment and achieving higher graduation rates in a cost-effective manner, even as their revenues per-student have declined."[12] What could these first-mover institutions learn from one another's experience? And what might be the takeaways for other schools?

The University Innovation Alliance, a group of eleven big public universities (including several that we'll look at), emerged from those conversations. Campus visits have spurred top administrators at these institutions to rethink their habitual ways of doing business. "The University of Texas [the state's flagship university] doesn't usually go to Georgia State," Tim Renick notes, "and the Alliance gives people in my position the opportunity to get honest appraisals of what does and doesn't work." Several of these universities are testing Georgia State's mini-grant model on their campuses and all of them are making smarter use of data analytics.

What matters most, the hope of expanding access is being realized—collectively, these universities are graduating 25 percent more Pell Grant–eligible students a year, with 100,000 additional low-income graduates projected by 2025.[13]

It's no surprise that Georgia State would willingly and widely share its best ideas, since it has opted out of the higher education rat-race. Despite being a national model for graduating more low-income students, it dropped thirty spots in the *U.S. News* rankings in 2017 because it refuses to play the selectivity game. "The university did literally the thing America needs all of higher education to do, and they got punished for it," Bridget Burns, who heads the Alliance, told *Politico*.[14]

I ask Mark Becker why, despite the fact that solutions like those developed at Georgia State—doable and affordable strategies that have been shown to reduce the dropout rate—are readily at hand, so few schools have accomplished much. "While college presidents talk the talk, they're not willing to make the changes necessary to do much about the problem," he responds.

Becker is infuriated by the unwillingness of so many college presidents to go to the mat for their students. "I can give you a social justice argument for ending the college dropout scandal and I can give you an economic one—ultimately, we can't have people rack up debt without getting a degree to show for it."

3

AGAINST THE ODDS

City University of New York and Rutgers University-Newark

"Can you simplify this square root?" Erica Fells asks her class, and a host of hands shoot up. All but one of the twenty-five students believe that, in this instance, it cannot be done. The dissenter, Leslie Alcantara, lays out her argument. "What do the rest of you think of Leslie's reasoning?" Ms. Fells asks, moving away from the blackboard, glasses perched on her nose, scanning the room. "Do you guys agree?"—and everyone wants to speak at once. After some back and forth they concur—Leslie is correct. Then Ms. Fells points to another square root that's a candidate for simplification. "You guys are great. Now what about this?" she asks, and once again the students clamor to respond.

In an ordinary college math class, the students are expected to memorize what's being spoon-fed to them and repeat the answers on the exam. Students in Ms. Fells's class must puzzle out the right answers for themselves, and only when they reach agreement does she move on.

CUNY: The Hands-On Approach

While this repartee sounds like a prep session for the GRE, which requires prospective graduate students to perform the same calculation, these students look nothing like the stereotype of the rollicking college student. Hostos Community College occupies several city blocks in what was once a tony enclave of the Bronx. The grandiosely named Grand Concourse borders the school, but while a handful of the ornate turn-of-the-century movie palaces survive, the neighborhood has turned into one of the poorest in the city.

This is the new-gen higher education world, where almost everyone is non-white and almost everyone receives federal and state aid earmarked for needy students. Like most new-gen undergraduates, community college is these students' entrée to higher education. Nationwide, poor students are three times more likely than their well-to-do classmates to start here. It's the collegiate home for half of all black and Latino freshmen but just a third of white students, and first-gen students are twice as likely to attend community college as those with college-educated parents.[1]

The students I met at Hostos are survivors—that's how they made it here—and most of them are juggling commitments that compete for scarce time. "At lunch I'm expressing breast milk and studying," A student I'll call Susanna G tells me. "I work full time, and my husband requires kidney dialysis." What they have accomplished in less than three months, as students in the break-the-mold program called CUNY Start, is almost beyond belief. At the outset of the semester, they were cowed by decimal points and negative numbers. Since then, they have powered through elementary school arithmetic to basic algebra, and now they are ready to tackle college-level math.

Another minor miracle is unfolding in Christopher Inniss's reading and writing class. There, students who initially had a hard time interpreting a short story are parsing the figurative language in a short story by the Trinidadian-British writer V. S. Naipaul that they might well read in freshman English. Inniss paces the classroom like a panther, using his voice as an instrument, cocking his head to listen. "How do you know?" he probes, whenever a student hazards an interpretation. "What's the evidence from the text?"

Plainly, what's happening in these CUNY Start classrooms holds some clues on how to solve the vexing problem of college dropouts.

Urban two-year colleges epitomize the dropout crisis at its worst. Nationwide, a student who goes to an inner-city community college like Hostos has only about a one-in-six chance of earning an associate degree.

The biggest stumbling blocks are remedial math, reading, and writing. More than two-thirds of all community college students must take at least one such class, and there they languish. Those in the trade favor the euphemism "developmental," but "dead end" is more apt—only a sixth of the students who take even a single remedial class wind up with an associate degree.[2]

At CUNY's community colleges, two-thirds of the students flunk at least one assessment exam.[3] Believing that they'll save time, since CUNY Start is a semester-long regimen of twenty five hours a week in class, most opt for old-school, one-semester remedial classes while simultaneously enrolling in college-level courses. But most of those students are making a consequential mistake. Although they may excel in their other classes, they still must pass the remedial courses in order to earn an associate degree, and they are less than half as likely to graduate in three years as their classmates who passed all the exams.[4]

By defying these odds, CUNY Start shows that students like those in Ms. Fells's and Mr. Inniss's classes are anything but hopeless causes. This amalgam of Socratic teaching, small classes, academic advising, and emotional backstopping represents a bold effort to solve an immense problem— prepping ill-prepared students to take college-level classes in English and math, and, eventually, earn an associate Associate's degree.

The success rate is phenomenal—75 percent of those who complete CUNY Start, nearly double the number who choose the memorize-the-formula remedial classes, pass the exams. That's unheard of in community college circles. "It's almost impossible to accomplish if a student is trying to get up to speed with regular remedial courses while also taking regular classes," observes Donna Linderman, the associate vice chancellor for academic affairs.

CUNY START: NO STRASBOURG-GOOSE-STYLE TEACHING

The CUNY Start model is simple to state, though devilishly hard to accomplish—fuse excellent teaching and a thought-evoking curriculum with I-have-your-back advising.

The teachers apprentice to veteran instructors before being handed their own classroom. Teachers generally report that they benefit greatly from in-the-classroom coaching, and these instructors have continuing support from coaches. The course materials are custom-made compilations, not off-the-shelf textbooks. Students are in class twenty-five hours a week, substantially more than the norm, for an entire semester. (Students who fail the assessment test in only one subject or those who cannot spend twenty-five hours in class can enroll part-time, taking a twelve-hour-a-week regimen.)[5]

"It's like an express train," Stefanie Rodriguez Balbuena says, describing her experience.

These students likely fell behind in elementary school and, as new concepts were introduced each year, they never caught up. The problem is particularly acute in math, where the all-too-familiar "Strasbourg goose" mode of teaching—stuff kids' heads with abstract formulas that bear no relation to the real world—left them convinced they were stupid. Old-school remedial classes deliver more of the same.

CUNY Start looks nothing like this. "We want them to be scientists, not memorizers," explains Steve Hinds, co-developer of the 650-page curriculum. "Our softly whispered goal is that we transform the way math education is done."

Steve Hinds isn't the only mathematician who harbors subversive thoughts about remedial education. As we have seen, Statway, which some CUNY instructors use in their college math classes, delivers the basics of math as well as the tools of college statistics in a year-long course. While these courses differ in their particulars, their underlying approach is the same—design a curriculum that demonstrates why math is worth studying; use a question-driven, rather than the conventional lecture-style, way of teaching; and give students the psychological tools that can make them more resilient.[6]

This is how Erica Fells runs her class. "Math isn't just memorization," she says. "I teach them how to investigate problems, how to think. The first sentence on the first day is a question. We start by making a connection to real life, and slowly build a foundation of knowledge for more abstract algebraic problems. I never say you are right or wrong. The answers come from them. I find something gifted in every student. One is good at answering questions, one is good at asking questions. My job as a teacher is to figure out what students are good at and allow them to shine. That's how they find their confidence."

"Erica helped me to have the courage to be the one against the class," says Leslie Alcantara. "You have to prove you are right and explain it."

Ms. Fells knows what her students are going through. "I grew up in the same neighborhood, attended the same schools. These students are as bright as students anyplace, but they don't believe it."

When she asks her class whether they think they're as intelligent as Columbia kids, they all say no. Although she pushes back, she understands why her students feel this way. "Over and over, they've gotten the message that they're inferior, told to forget about going to college because they're 'not college material.'" When she was a high school freshman, one girl was urged by her counselor to drop out. "You're just going to get pregnant by the time you're sixteen. Why waste everybody's time by staying in school?"

These teachers do everything in their power to help the students grasp their own potential. By setting high standards and rewarding effort, they foster a growth mindset. They urge students who are floundering to work with tutors who themselves went through CUNY Start and are now enrolled full-time at Hostos. They discard the mask of the impersonal, letting their class know that they faced their own insecurities when they were their age. "Students get that you're a person too," explains Christopher Innis, the reading and writing instructor. "That allows me to push: 'I need more.'"

"Our teachers aren't just filling a role," says Leslie Alcantara. "They live it, eat it, breathe it."

The teachers' job is to motivate their students so that they can pass the assessment exams. The CUNY Start advisers have a complementary responsibility—they invite students to talk candidly about the sometimes-harrowing events in their lives. "The students aren't comfortable letting their teachers know about the court date, the pending eviction, the abusive foster parent," says Jessica Mingus, the CUNY Start director at Hostos. "The adviser tells them: 'I want to know about you—not just the pretty stuff.'"

The message that students get—one that they may never have heard before—is that someone cares about them, that Hostos feels like home. As we've seen, psychologists have demonstrated that students need to grasp that they belong in college—that they aren't imposters.[7]

It's impossible to overstate the momentousness of acquiring a sense of belonging for students like these, who may never have had a place they could truly call home or a person who listened to them. "When they're down, these students say they're not cut out for this," Ms. Mingus tells me, "they see themselves as imposters. We remind them that they passed their New York State Regents exams [required to graduate from high school], sometimes after as many as five tries. We tell them that's a great accomplishment, and you can do the same here."

Asked to write about the ups and downs in their lives, many of the students matter-of-factly describe acts of violence, abandonment, abuse, and thoughts of committing suicide. "Sex experience with a family member" and "guns fired all the time," one reports, detailing events that occurred when she was still in elementary school. In middle school, she adds, she had a miscarriage, joined a gang, and wound up in jail. "Life is not a VCR," another writes. "You can't rewind it." Profiles in courage—the scars won't go away, but the fact that these students have made it to college means that it is possible to construct a new life for themselves.

Ms. Mingus has a boatload of stories about CUNY Start graduates who made striking changes in their lives. Cynthia, an undocumented Chinese student, didn't say a word in class for the first month of the program. She was too embarrassed by her accent to speak, but after lots of coaching, she ginned up the courage to stand up in class and ask her classmates if she could join a study group. Eventually she found her cause—giving "Dreamers" the opportunity to go to college—and wound up being asked to testify about the issue before the New York City Council and a New York State Assembly committee. She has also become more ambitious—instead of being a dental hygienist, her initial goal, she has her sights set on a career in law. And then there's Alex, who went to jail as a teenager—"he never discussed what he did, and we never asked him," says Ms. Mingus—and scraped through high school with a GED. After CUNY Start, Alex earned his associate degree and transferred to John Jay College, one of the most selective four-year schools in the CUNY system. "No one expected me to amount to anything," he told Ms. Mingus, "but there were a bunch of [CUNY Start] people in my corner."

"We become therapists—empowering voices and planting seeds," Ms. Mingus tells me. "Then we get to see the transformation."

ASAP: "The People's College"

Community college was envisioned by its Progressive Era founders as a noble democratic experiment—the "people's college," which would deliver an affordable, open-to-all entrée into higher learning, until then the preserve of the gentility, to working-class Americans. During the second half of the twentieth century, as more and more of these colleges expanded, they formulated a revolutionary open-admissions policy.[8]

Anyone with a high school diploma or GED degree can enroll in one of CUNY's seven community colleges. But fewer than a quarter of these students make it to graduation.

ASAP, the Accelerated Study in Associate Programs, delivers a CARE package calculated to address the likely causes of this failure, helping students surmount the array of financial, academic, and personal obstacles that bedevil them.[9]

ASAP blankets students with assistance that includes transit passes and textbook subsidies; carefully crafted pathways to a degree; compact course schedules that leave chunks of time for home and work; and, critically, a hefty dose of personal, high-touch advising.[10]

Almost all these students come from low-income families, and money woes can force them to leave school. In 2017, New York tackled this problem by guaranteeing that full-time students from poor and middle-class families don't pay tuition.[11] ASAP goes further, giving them free public transportation passes—that's $121 a month saved—as well as defraying the thousand-dollar-a-year cost of textbooks. While these students must take a full course load, since research shows that full-time students are far more likely to graduate than part-timers, their class schedule is consolidated, which makes it easier for them to balance the rigors of college with the necessity of earning money and caring for members of their family.[12]

Community colleges operate on a pittance, compared to four-year schools. Most cannot afford the person-to-person guidance that will help these students thrive, and each adviser may be assigned as many as two thousand students. But as we've seen, knowledgeable advising has a powerful impact on student success, which is why ASAP has invested heavily in this type of support.[13]

Some students say they were enticed into signing up for ASAP because of the free transit passes, but a survey found that what they value the most is the bond with their advisers. "I told my adviser what I am interested in and she said 'that sounds like sociology,'" says a student I'll call Mary S. "I never heard of sociology, but I tried it out, and now it's my major." Another student, Pablo E., took remedial math six times before finally passing. "If my adviser wasn't pushing me I would have quit long ago."

As with CUNY Start, these students have someone to talk with about what's happening outside the classroom. "Single mom, all of it, I come here and say I can't do it any more, they tell me I can't quit," Mary S. tells me. "Having my adviser say, 'you're not the only one, other students are getting through it'—that keeps me going. My adviser is my therapist, she psychoanalyzes me all the time."

"I don't think ASAP is a program," adds Alyssa R. "It's a family. I have a place that I belong to, people that support me."[14]

Here's why this model warrants nationwide attention—every year since ASAP was launched, a decade ago, more than half the students have earned an associate degree in three years. That's more than double the percentage of a matched group of students who didn't participate. And while the program keeps getting bigger, there has been no diminution in quality—indeed, the percentage of ASAP graduates has increased slightly.

There's more good news to report. Students who had enrolled in CUNY Start are just as likely to graduate as the rest of the ASAP students. Most of these undergraduates continue with their education after getting their associate degree. And African American male students, usually the likeliest to drop out of college, are earning associate degrees at almost the same rate as the average ASAP student.[15]

"We're always being asked, 'What's the most important factor—what's ASAP's secret sauce?' but I tell them that there is no secret sauce," Donna Linderman says. "Each part of the model, like advising or free tuition, hasn't moved the needle when it has been tried by itself. In order to get results you need the whole package."

"At CUNY, we live or die by the research," she adds. MDRC, a highly-regarded social policy research firm, conducted a randomized-control trial of ASAP. Academic researchers, who study everything under the sun, do a terrible job of studying their own institutions. This is the most rigorous study of any large-scale higher education initiative, and the results confirm Ms. Linderman's view that that this multipronged model works.[16]

The essence of the CUNY initiative—like the honors college at Rutgers University-Newark that prizes grit over grades, which we'll visit next—is straightforward: give students the attention and care akin to what's lavished on those who go to top-ranked universities and they will flourish.

At schools like Harvard University and Amherst College, our final stop, upwards of 90 percent of the undergraduates earn a bachelor's degree. While these students may well be among the best and brightest, they also get kid-glove treatment. If they run into trouble, a gaggle of counselors, advisers, and tutors stands at the ready. Think of what the elite institutions are doing as the Rolls Royce model and ASAP as the Honda Civic—although it has far fewer bells and whistles, it runs smoothly. Put another way, these CUNY strategies provide Harvard-style support, adapted for mass higher education.

These programs don't come cheap—the semester-long CUNY Start program costs about $2,100 per student, ASAP about $3,500 a year extra—but they more than pay for themselves. Economists Henry Levin, at Columbia, and Emma Garcia, at the Economic Policy Institute and Georgetown, have shown that every dollar invested in ASAP by taxpayers generates $3.50 because of increased earnings. Enrolling a thousand students in ASAP brings $46 million more benefits to students and taxpayers than admitting the same number of students and not giving them this additional support.[17]

Over the long term, students who enroll in ASAP are big gainers as well. Research shows they are much less likely to wind up in prison or on welfare, and they report that they are healthier and happier. They're more likely to participate in politics and volunteer at nonprofits. The degree brings better job prospects and an income that's 25 percent higher than the average college dropout.[18] This is precisely what the "People's Colleges" are meant to do.[19]

Getting Bigger and Going National

The idea for ASAP came from former CUNY chancellor Matthew Goldstein, a font of innovation.

Here's the story he shares with me. "I was in bed, my wife was in bed beside me, when I got up and started walking around. 'Are you okay?' she asked. I said: 'I'm just thinking about community colleges.'" The chancellor had introduced what he characterizes as "a number of controversial initiatives" in the four-year colleges, "but the one area I felt unsure about was the community colleges."

"I became a little upset. I understood that, yes, these students weren't as well prepared as students entering a bachelor's program. I understood that many of them had to make choices between going to work and going to school. I understood that many were single parents. But I could not understand graduation rates in the teens.

"I said to myself—this was all in my head—that one thing I could do was to take the uncertainty out of the system. These young people have no roadmap for navigating a complex institution. They're asked as soon as they walk in what they are going to major in. They're worried about registering for classes, balancing school with a job in the evenings. If I can soften these knotty points that could change graduation rates."

The thoughts kept coming. "If I'm going to minimize uncertainty, why not block programs, so students would have regular hours to work or be with their kids. If they are having problems between choosing to pay for a bus or paying for school or buying a slice of pizza, let's give them Metrocards. Let's have books paid for.

"I called [former mayor Michael] Bloomberg, with whom I had a great relationship. I described my vision and he said, 'If you have the money to implement these ideas, what do you think your graduation rates would be after three years?' I looked him in the eye and took a deep breath and said we could probably get graduation rates to over 50 percent. That was more than three times what we were doing but I had a gut feeling that if we had the money to invest we would really have a good shot. Bloomberg asked how much I needed. I said twenty million. He said: 'You got it.'" As things turned out, Goldstein made good on his pledge to the mayor.

In New York City, programs that prove themselves expand rapidly, and that has been true for ASAP. With $83.5 million from Mayor Bill de Blasio, it now reaches twenty-five thousand students—that's half of the community college students who enroll full time.

Educators elsewhere are paying heed. With technical support from the ASAP staff, community colleges in upstate New York, Ohio, and California have copied the model, and several more states are poised to do the same.

Those states may be motivated to act by the findings of a 2018 MDRC evaluation of the Ohio's ASAP-style initiative. The bottom line is the same—in Ohio, as in New York, the program has more than doubled the community college's graduation rate. What makes this result especially impressive is the fact that these students were older than their ASAP counterparts, more likely to be parents and twice as likely to be working. "The successful adaptation of the City University of New York's ASAP program in Ohio is remarkable because it shows that the model can achieve great results in new contexts and with different types of students," MDRC president Gordon Berlin points out. It's an exemplar of success that merits emulation nationwide.[20]

What's more, there's every reason to believe that, while ASAP was developed for community college students, the same approach will work equally well at any four-year institution that's contending with its own dropout crisis. This proposition is currently being tested in New York City, where the model was introduced at John Jay College of Criminal Justice, one of CUNY's four-year institutions, in 2015. The school is on track to double its four-year graduation rate.

"I would love to have the ASAP model adopted system-wide," says Matthew Goldstein. "If you can save one out of two students who start at a community college, as opposed to one out of five, that will lead to more jobs, better-paying jobs, people living better lives."

Rutgers University-Newark: Honors for Grit, Not Grades

University leaders who crave national recognition give pride of place to research, and the first thing you're likely to hear about on those campuses is the tens of millions of dollars in grants they have been awarded. Undergraduates are an afterthought in these schools. "For a research institution, we do a good job," a senior administrator at Berkeley, where I teach, once told me, when I inquired about the uneven quality of instruction.

Rutgers University-Newark has opted for a very different approach. The school has made diversity its calling card, and for the past eighteen years, U.S. News has hailed it as the nation's most diverse university. "We have the talent pool to change the shape of the country, the next generation of change-makers," boasts President Nancy Cantor. The school is doing well by doing good—two-thirds of the undergraduates earn a bachelor's degree in six years, 15 percentage points higher than schools with similar demographics, and there's a negligible difference in the graduation rate for new-gen students.

The city of Newark, whose stock plummeted after the 1967 rebellion, is coming back, and the university has formed ties with City Hall and local businesses to promote its "Hire Buy Live Newark" initiative. Since Cantor became president, in 2014, the number of Newark students has grown by 60 percent. The university now guarantees a free ride to graduates of local high schools and New Jersey community colleges whose families earn less than $60,000, attracting poor and working-class students who otherwise couldn't afford the tab.

When you talk with Nancy Cantor, the Honors Live-Learn Community is what you hear about first. With good reason—with its emphasis on grit and not grades, and with students who look more like those at CUNY than the standard-issue undergraduate, the venture is reinventing the idea of an honors college. And like the CUNY initiatives, the success of Rutgers's approach confirms the value of enabling students to understand that they are full-fledged members of a caring community—that they belong.

UPENDING THE HONORS COLLEGE MODEL

Tyreek works full-time in the sanitation department while co-parenting his ten-year-old son. Ahjoni, a cancer survivor, endured a chemotherapy regimen. Mohamed was kicked out of a Muslim prep school, then repeatedly suspended from high school for, among other things, selling chocolate to his classmates. Emanuel was serving a three-year sentence for armed robbery when a jury tossed out his conviction. These are hardly the profiles of typical honors college students, but they are all enrolled in the Rutgers program.

Nationwide, the drive for status has generated an explosion in the number of honors colleges. Nearly nine hundred schools—60 percent more than in 2000—belong to the National Collegiate Honors Council. It's a coup for these institutions, almost all of them public universities and community colleges, to snare applicants whose top-of-the-class high school records and SAT scores would ensure them a place at a renowned private college. The bait is the honors college, which promises them the intimate feel of a small college amid an outsized institution.

"Many provosts and presidents see honors colleges as a way to attract students who will raise the school's average GPA and test scores," explains Loyola University of New Orleans professor Naomi Yavneh, the president of the honors organization. "Equity is too often left out of the conversation." These students, mostly white and middle class, receive concierge treatment, with sizable scholarships, separate housing, special seminars, faculty mentors, research opportunities, and first crack at courses in high demand.[21]

Unlike other honors colleges, the Rutgers Honors Living Learning Community is mainly composed of black and Latino students, mostly from Newark and the neighboring towns. Nearly half of them are the first in their family to go to college, and three-quarters are eligible for federal Pell Grants. Their high school grades and SAT scores are lower than the campus average. Few universities would have awarded them scholarships, let alone enrolled them in a hand-tailored academic program, but at Rutgers they get white-glove treatment because of their potential as leaders.

While high school grades are taken into account in determining who gets selected, the emphasis is on their resiliency, their drive to learn, and their passion for social justice. "The selection process itself highly engages the students even before orientation begins," Vice Chancellor John Gunkel points out. "Starting earlier helps these students invest in themselves in a way that offsets the disconnectedness that many institutions struggle against. And everyone who participates in the process buys in to what happens with the students, creating a real community of student support."

Each element of the model comes straight from the book on how to engage undergraduates in general and minority students in particular. The students are given scholarships that cover both tuition and living expenses. Without this aid, most of them couldn't enroll full-time and, as we've observed at CUNY, part-time students are much more likely to drop out. Nearly half are community college graduates, because the designers of the model thought eighteen-year-olds should have the chance to learn from classmates with greater life experience. Some professors opposed at this arrangement, arguing that students who had gone to community college weren't as bright as newly-minted high school graduates, but they have been proven wrong. These students are faring as well as their classmates.

Seminars in the honors program, which range from civil rights to environmental justice, put community engagement and social justice front and center. These are high-expectations classes that demand more reading and writing than Rutgers undergraduates usually encounter. They are designed to connect what's happening locally to the wider world. The students in a marketing course work for a company that's promoting the "Hire Buy Live Newark" initiative and an art course delves into the lives of Portuguese immigrants. Junius Williams—a leading light in the honors program, idolized by the students I talked with—spent more than four decades as a public school advocate, lawyer, and grass-roots organizer in Newark.

"For the first time these students are learning about themselves and about the city where they come from," says Dean Englebert Santana.

Insights about the value of instilling a sense of belonging and a growth mindset underlie the stress placed on forging personal bonds. If their classes threaten to sink them or their real-life issues overwhelm them, they are sustained by what one student describes as "multiple check-ins." They can turn to a peer mentor who may well have struggled through a similar experience. They can meet with one of the deans, who know them on a first-name basis, and they can repair to their faculty adviser.

"The adviser is there to identify red flags—whether it's finances, academics, or personal," Dean Santana tells me. "That means helping a student with a full-time job who's majoring in biology deal with anxiety or helping a student get out of a toxic relationship." Law professor Taji-Nia Henderson believes that "if we hadn't been there, the students wouldn't have made it. They keep saying: 'I don't have anyone else to talk to about this.' "

"The amount we get from everyone—classmates, faculty, administration, faculty—is mind-blowing," says Adebimpe Elegbeleye, a student from Nigeria. "The nurturing environment allows us to come to our full potential. I never thought that college could be like this. When I talk to friends at other universities and tell them what's going on, they say, 'Wow, you know this dean? You have what support?' "

"Initially, I was embarrassed to be part of the program. It felt like a lackluster attempt to rescue inner-city kids from failing high schools and call them 'honor students' to make them feel better," reveals Mohamed Abdelghany. He's the student who was perpetually being suspended from high school. He changed his mind, though, once he came to know his classmates. "These students are brilliant in their own way, but they did not have the tools or the support to build the best version of themselves. It's a humbling experience when a group of people believe in you and your potential when you can't see it." A star debater and a member of the student government while at Rutgers, he is now at Harvard Law School.

Although this program doesn't come cheap, the $37,000 per-student cost to the university is 40 percent less than what Harvard charges for tuition, room and board. The data indicates that the university is making a sensible bet. Despite the fact that these students fared worse in high school than the typical Rutgers-Newark freshmen, their B+ GPA is half a grade higher than the university average. Fifteen percent of Rutgers students drop out after their first year, but no-one in the honors program has quit college.

"This is a lab where new ideas can be tried out," Dean Timothy Eatman says, and universities that are reconsidering the premises of an honors college can learn a lot from this venture. As Naomi Yavneh notes, "honors students from first-generation and other less traditional backgrounds are more likely to stay in school and graduate from honors because the high-impact practices we do in honors are of special benefit to students from marginalized populations."

THE POWER OF THE PERSONAL

Here's the big takeaway from CUNY and Rutgers-Newark—the power of the personal is the make-or-break factor.

The Rutgers Honors Living Learning Community shows that undergraduates who other universities wouldn't give a second thought to will thrive if they get the kind of attention their peers at more prestigious places take for granted. CUNY Start demonstrates that, with the right combination of a mindset-centered curriculum and caring counseling, students who start out with bare-bones math and reading skills can become ready for college in a single semester. And CUNY's ASAP program is proof that graduation rates can markedly rise when students are buoyed by supports.

Imagine the impact if strategies like these went nationwide.[22]

4

UNIVERSITY OF CENTRAL FLORIDA AND VALENCIA COLLEGE
The Power of Two

The camera loves Angel Sanchez. The recent University of Central Florida graduate has the incandescent thousand-watt smile, razor-sharp haircut, well-tailored suit, and confident demeanor of someone whose photo you might find in a college promo. His academic credentials are even more impressive—a 4.0 GPA; a pair of judicial clerkships; a coauthored law review article; and a ticket to law school, with a fat scholarship from the Jack Kent Cooke Foundation and a career in criminal justice.

But what the photo and the CV don't reveal is that, before he went to college, Angel Sanchez spent nine years in prison for attempted murder.[1]

"I grew up in Miami's Little Havana," Angel tells me. "Starting in elementary school I ran with gangs. My dad was always preaching the value of an education, but I was behind bars most of the time, in juvie by age twelve, and then jail." When he was sixteen, he was convicted of attempted murder, in a clash between rival gangs, and given a thirty-year prison sentence.

"You have a lot of time to think when you're in prison. It politicized me and made me yearn for an education." A *USA Today* article about the All-Academic Community College Team was an eye-opener. "They were all second-chance people, people who've crashed and come back," he says. "I decided right there that I was going to find a community college and I'm going to make this USA All-Academic Team."

Angel earned his GED and a paralegal certificate, which secured him a job in the prison law library. He started reading Florida Supreme Court cases, and when he came across an opinion that tossed out the harsh guidelines for his prison sentence, he saw his chance. He found lawyers to go to bat for him, and after twelve years behind bars, he was a free man.

"I'm twenty-eight going on seventeen," Angel says, remembering that moment. "My experience is that the world thinks I'm the scum of the earth." He began contacting community colleges across the state, inquiring whether he could enroll after he was released. Most schools sent him form letters or catalogs, but the Valencia College catalog came with a Post-It note attached: "Come see us when you get out." Those six words meant everything to him. "I would have been happy if they sent a student handbook. But they sent a note!"

Orlando, where Valencia College and the University of Central Florida are located, was as far north as he dared to venture. "I thought it snowed here," he recalls. He couldn't believe that the college wanted him to come. "I said, 'Are you serious, there's someone in the world who's not afraid to welcome me?'" Looking for a place to live, with no money for rent, he caught a break at the homeless shelter run by the Salvation Army. The shelter usually houses men looking for a full-time job, a jump-start to a new life, but it made an exception for someone so eager to return to school, and Angel lived there for the next year and a half.

"I started out as a remedial student—I'd never studied algebra—but I was hungry to learn. Professors get excited to see a kid who has the drive." Quickly, his education took off. He earned straight As and was invited to join Valencia's honors college, with its smaller classes and earmarked scholarships.

Angel could afford college only because Florida waives tuition for homeless students, and the plight of these "invisible students" became his cause. At a panel discussion at Valencia that featured Jill Biden, he spoke up, urging other states to follow Florida's example. Sandy Shugart, the president of

Valencia, came up to him after the event. "I was nervous," Angel tells me, "maybe I'd done something wrong, but he hugged me and took me to lunch. He's become a real friend. He's always been willing to vouch for me."

From convict to model student—Angel graduated from Valencia with a 4.0 GPA. "We don't settle, we succeed," he exhorted his classmates at commencement.

The University of Central Florida, where he transferred for his bachelor's degree, presented him with a new set of difficulties. Academic standards were higher, classes much bigger, and professors less accessible. "There's a lot less handholding than Valencia," he says. Angel, a master at forging connections, reached out to several professors, asking if he could work with them on a research project. "I didn't know what research was, but I knew I wanted to do it."

When Florida legislators interviewed Angel, they saw a narrative of re-demption, and he spent a semester interning in Tallahassee. Back on campus, he kept busy, working with the Washington, DC–based Campaign for Youth Justice on juvenile justice reform and organizing a book drive for the local jail. "He's the hardest-working student I've ever taught," says Cynthia Schmidt, a legal studies lecturer and moot court coach. "In his first year of moot court, he didn't make it past the first day of the regional com-petition. In his second year, he placed fifth in the nation. He has re-identified himself as a scholar."

In 2017, Angel graduated from UCF with a straight-A average in po-litical science and legal studies. He enrolled that fall at the University of Miami Law School, aiming to use the tools of the law to promote social justice. "I look back and see individuals who vouched for me. They have changed a cookie-cutter system to make it a system that looks at people, one by one."

Hang Together or Hang Separately

Angel Sanchez's story echoes the classic Horatio Alger rags-to-riches tale, updated for our times. But it is so much more than the plot line for an afterschool special about how, against stiff odds, one resilient individual made a new life for himself. Every year, more than six thousand students, many with sketchy backgrounds, make the same journey across the city of Orlando.

"That kid that everyone else has written off, that Angel, he has something amazing in him," Sandy Shugart tells me. "Our job is to recognize what that 'something' is. And there are thousands like him."

Valencia College and the University of Central Florida are upstarts in the staid world of higher education. They opened their doors barely half a century ago, with little fanfare and modest expectations, and have been growing exponentially—the University of Central Florida enrolls sixty-six thousand students and Valencia seventy-five thousand, making them among the nation's biggest institutions of higher learning. "We do recognize there is a limit," says UCF's former president, John Hitt. "We just don't know what it is." The Aspen Institute singled out Valencia College as the nation's best community college in 2012, the first such award made by the Institute; *U.S. News* named UCF as among the nation's most innovative universities; and *Washington Monthly* ranked Hitt and Shugart among the country's ten most inventive college presidents.[2]

Hang together or hang separately—what makes these schools especially noteworthy, and worthy of emulation, is the first-in-nation guarantee that every Valencia College graduate can go straight to the University of Central Florida. Half of the university's graduates come via this route, called DirectConnect. Students who scraped through high school, and who might otherwise have wound up wearing Mickey Mouse costumes at nearby Disneyworld, are making the grade.

Ivy League colleges wear their exclusivity like a badge of honor, touting how many applicants they reject. The experience of the University of Central Florida shows that a university can be both big and good.

A lot of institutions are proud of who they don't accept," John Hitt observes. "We're proud of who we can accept."[3]

"It's a rare sight to see institutions self-consciously trying to build capacity to serve more students," Andrew Kelly, a higher education analyst at the American Enterprise Institute, told a *Washington Post* reporter. "The incentives tend to point in the opposite direction. These guys are breaking the mold."[4]

Valencia College—"Everyone Can Learn Anything under the Right Conditions"

Sandy Shugart was on an airplane, musing as he often does about how Valencia could be doing a better job, when he had a brainstorm—most of the students never had the chance to explore what they wanted to make of their lives. Some are couch-surfers, getting by on a meal or two a day; some speak barebones English; and some perpetually wonder whether they will be deported. That they made it to campus is itself remarkable.

Some top-notch students come to Valencia in order to save money, getting a solid two years of college education there before transferring to a university. But most of these undergraduates barely eked out a high school degree. They arrive with narrow ambitions and pinched horizons. Audacious options are not off the table—they have never surfaced. "They think that 'people like me don't do X,'" says Joyce Romano, the vice president for student affairs.

These undergraduates deserve the chance to embark on a journey of self-discovery, Shugart thought, and out of this insight was born a course called the New Student Experience. As is often the case, the president encapsulated his thinking in a catchy phrase—"the Six Ps": purpose, pathways, plan, preparation, personal connection, and place.

This way of thinking encapsulates Sandy Shugart's style of leadership. He has been the president of Valencia since 2000, and every one of what are known as the Big Ideas—sweeping conceptualizations, rooted in evidence, that propel the college to design an improved experience for the students— has given deeper meaning to the concept of a "student-centered" institution.[5] In paying tribute to the college, the Aspen Institute made much of its "unique culture of continuous improvement and innovation. The impact on student outcomes is amazing to see."

Valencia College was launched in 1967, with a few hundred students crammed into twenty trailers on a muddy parking lot. Orlando's power brokers had waged a "segregation now, segregation forever" campaign to keep the school from opening, preferring a private college for "white Christians" over an integrated public institution. "Valencia had the longest gestation period of any of Florida's community colleges," Lee Henderson of the Florida Department of Education recalls. "But maybe that wasn't all bad, because when it finally came into being it came as one of the finest in the country."[6]

Valencia was slow to realize its potential. As is the case at many similar institutions, the dropout rate was sky-high and the transfer rate dispiritingly low. Paul Gianini, Sandy Shugart's predecessor, was "very good at pinching the pennies," Shugart recounts. "The College was organized around an implicit manufacturing model—put lots of raw material in one end, get product out the other. This was manufacturing at scale, and students weren't treated in deep personal ways. But as long as business outcomes trump everything else, there are real limits to improving student outcomes. I came in to unseat that.

"What changed? Damn near everything."

"We may do some things that cost us revenue and enrollment in the short term but we'll increase learning in the long term," Shugart announced to the faculty and administrators in his first address. "What if we make Valencia the learning college for the twenty-first century?"

First on Shugart's Big Ideas list is the proposition that "everyone can learn anything under the right conditions. Our students have all the biological gifts, the inherent capabilities to learn anything we teach." This assertion flies in the face of the widely held belief that students with spotty high school records aren't "college material," shifting the focus from "the deficiencies of the learner to the conditions of learning."[7]

"There's no reason why students of different income levels and ethnicities should do any differently, success-wise, around here," Shugart contended. "Our students can perform as well as any others in the country, at any institution, given the right supports."

For Valencia graduate Wilfredo Ortiz, this encouragement made all the difference. "I was twenty-eight and a convicted felon. I knew it would be a challenge getting back in the swing of things. I was surrounded by some of the most supportive people I could ever meet, regardless of the mistakes I had made." He majored in engineering, graduated with a near-perfect GPA, earned a bachelor's degree from UCF, and got an engineering job at nearby Lockheed Martin.

"Will student learning be improved? How do we know?"—at Valencia, that is the metric for every decision affecting students.[8] "If learning is there, it's going to be reflected in the outcomes," says Shugart. Seminar-size classes (the average size is twenty-three) enable teachers to know their students personally, not simply as names on exam papers. Give-and-take pedagogy, rather than lectures, keeps students in the game.

"Programs Are Merely the Vessels, People Are the Wine"

"Start Right" is on the Big Ideas list because the "front door," the first semester of college, is the make-or-break time for most community college students. Data-mining showed that Valencia freshmen who passed their first five courses were three times more likely to graduate than those who passed only three. That's why assessment, advising, and placement all occur before the first class. It is also why the school doesn't let students engage in course-shopping, switching in and out of classes, once the term has begun.

"We wanted to recapture the first two weeks of instruction," says Shugart. "I made a deal with the faculty—if we do this [adopt a no-drop, no-add rule], you need to make the first minute of the first meeting of the first class a learning minute. "

"Students have to make lots of important decisions and at many community colleges they are pretty much on their own," Tom Bailey, the President of Teachers College, Columbia University and author of *Redesigning America's Community Colleges*, points out. "That's why we call this the cafeteria college: There's a lot of stuff there, but students end up with a lot of wheel-spinning."[9] By contrast, students at Valencia, working with an adviser, map a path to graduation and beyond during their first semester.

As is the case at every high-performing college I visited, the bond between students and their professors and advisers matters the most at Valencia, especially for those who arrive ill prepared to do college-level work. Shugart tells me that "when a renowned researcher asked five very different students who had succeeded against the odds what had made the difference to them, each gave essentially the same answer—they all named people who had taken a strong interest in their learning.

"Our programs are merely vessels. The people who work in them are the wine."[10]

This philosophy underlies the New Student Experience course. Like many of her classmates, Nardia Hodge arrived on campus uncertain whether she could handle college-level work. "I left that class with something I wasn't expecting—a change in myself," she says. "I knew I wanted to be a business-woman, but a lot has changed about what I thought I wanted in my education and career plans."

Chip Turner, who teaches the course, hears this sentiment all the time. "We explore who these students are—What's meaningful? What can they do that will benefit the greater good as well as themselves?"—then join this sense of purpose to a vocation and a way to get from here to there. It's an opportunity to dive deep—students have to rethink everything. One freshman was positive that he'd be a nurse, which is what his father and mother did, but after shadowing a nurse he concluded that nursing wasn't a good fit for him.

In their final assignment, the students are asked to imagine that it's a decade into the future—What are you doing? What steps did you take to get here? "This brings to life the work they have done. It helps them make more sense of 'career.' It's a reality check, their 'aha! moment,'" says Turner. In his back-to-the-future presentation, the student bent on being a nurse spoke about what he had gleaned from the course. "'I thought it was going to be a waste of time, because I knew that I wanted to be a nurse, but I realized that being a nurse isn't what I want to do.'"

Those who teach the New Student Experience course double as advisers for the students in their first seminar. "These students want someone who will listen to them, and I have a great ear for listening," says Turner. One of his students was distraught because not having a car made her miss the classes she loved. A woman transitioning to being a male barged into his office, livid that "'they still think of me as a female. They won't recognize me as who I am.'"

Teaching, Not Research, Is Priority #1

"The college is how the students experience us" is another Valencia Big Idea, which is why so much attention gets devoted to what's happening in classrooms. I stopped by at a poster event, where students presented projects they worked on with professors. So did faculty members, but rather than describe research in their discipline, as you'd expect, their presentations described a new classroom strategy. Sandra Bowling constructed real-world problems to demonstrate the practical applications of trigonometry, and Randy Gordon found a novel way to show budding writers how to move smoothly from text to quotation.[11]

When academics revamp a course, they almost never consider it a topic for research. But these professors developed quantifiable measures to determine whether their innovations improved students' outcomes. In both instances, the answer was "yes"— when the math students' performance was compared to the previous year's class, 50 percent more of them could solve the trigonometry problems; and when students were tested before and after the writing project, 89 percent had learned how to tie quotes to their own writing.

Publishing in peer-reviewed journals and university presses comes first for university professors, since research is the main criterion for promotion and tenure, and teaching takes a back seat. Professors whose classroom performance is judged "good enough" get rewarded if their research is stellar, while superb teachers are shown the door if their research doesn't impress reviewers. Most faculty at four-year institutions are never taught how to teach, which may explain why 94 percent of them believe that they're wizards in the classroom but their colleagues' performance leaves much to be desired.[12]

Community college instructors, by contrast, are devoted to their students, and teaching is what counts. Every candidate for tenure at Valencia must follow Sandra Bowling's and Randy Gordon's examples, testing new ideas in the classroom and appraising their effectiveness. The effective innovations are spread across the college.

"We have mountains of work to do to get faculty to agree on learning outcomes for their classes," says Shugart. "If you come in May, you'd have 200 faculty on the clock, thinking about learning outcomes and how they align to outcomes in the next course. This is the stuff that bores our board members, but it's the real work. 'How do I know if they learn?'"

The president's hunch about value of the New Student Experience class proved to be on the money. The new course was motivated by his sense that letting students' imaginations roam free would encourage them to stay in school beyond their first semester, when the likelihood of dropping out is greatest. That's what happened—students often leave community college after a semester; in the first year that the course was offered, 10 percent more of them remained in the spring term.

Half of Valencia's students graduate or transfer in three years—by comparison, across the community college landscape, only 39 percent earn a degree in double that amount of time—and while graduation rates have flattened at two-year schools, they keep rising at Valencia. The college ranks fourth, nationwide, among community colleges in the number of Latino graduates and sixth in the number of African-American graduates. It has the highest graduation rate, the highest salaries after graduation, and the highest transfer rate among Florida's two-year schools.[13] It operates on a pittance—$3,000 a student, which is about 3 percent of what Harvard spends—which makes its accomplishments even more remarkable. (I asked Shugart how he could do so much on so little: "First rule is don't whine. Scarcity is no excuse for poor performance.")[14]

Sandy Shugart isn't satisfied. "I want to see a 60 percent graduation rate. I think that's doable before I die." Meanwhile, the students couldn't be happier with their experience. On a website called "Rate My Professor," undergraduates hand out kudos and brickbats about their campus and their professors. Valencia ranks second nationwide.[15]

"Community colleges get a bad rap," Wilfredo Ortiztells me. "They call it the thirteenth grade, but you get a really good education here."

THE UNIVERSITY OF CENTRAL FLORIDA—BIGGER AND BETTER

Can a rapidly expanding public university deliver a first-class education on a skinflint budget? The University of Central Florida, like many state schools, faces this dilemma, and almost every university president contends that it cannot be done. An influx of money is imperative, they contend, if their institutions are going to fulfill their mission.[16]

After interviewing a host of presidents, Public Agenda and the National Center for Public Policy and Higher Education concluded that "the three main factors in higher education—cost, quality, and access—exist in what we call an iron triangle. These factors are linked in an unbreakable reciprocal relationship, such that any change in one will inevitably impact the others. Most of the presidents believe that if one wants to improve the quality of higher education, one must either put more money in the system or be prepared to see higher education become less accessible to students. Conversely, cutting costs in higher education must eventually lead to cuts either in quality or access."[17]

The University of Central Florida has figured out how extricate itself from the iron triangle. A state-of-the-art online education program, coupled with the pipeline of good upperclassmen through DirectConnect, have enabled it to maintain quality and expand access while keeping its costs low.

On November 22, 1963 (as it happens, the day President Kennedy was shot), Walt Disney flew over south-central Florida, scouting for the site of an East Coast Disneyland. When he stared down at the barren, swampy terrain of Orange County, bisected by interstate highways, he knew he had found the right location.

Disney's decision transformed Orlando from a sleepy city whose claim to fame was a nearby air force base to the mid-twentieth-century version of the gold rush. Disneyworld turned into a franchise, and a bevy of theme parks followed, until Orlando boasted more palaces of amusement than anywhere else in the world. Overnight, the city became the nation's fastest-growing metropolitan region. What it lacked was a university.

The city fathers had Space U in mind, a vision lifted from the Jetsons, and the original mission of Florida Technical University, which opened in 1965, was training workers for the space program. The school changed its name to the University of Central Florida in 1975, growing steadily and broadening its offerings, but for the next three decades it remained a commuter school of no special distinction. The standing joke was that its initials stood for "U Can't Finish."

When John Hitt became president in 1992, Orlando was booming but Florida's public universities weren't meeting the burgeoning student demand. The University of Florida, the state's flagship school, expanded by just 1 percent while the population was growing twenty times faster. The University of Central Florida has filled the vacuum, growing with the velocity of a startup while maturing into a well-regarded academic institution. "We didn't take shortcuts to speed up scaling," Hitt tells me. "We kept the focus on teaching and learning."

UCF has tripled in size since John Hitt took the reins—it enrolls as many undergraduates as the entire Ivy League—while stiffening its admissions standards. Nearly 70 percent of the students graduate within six years, 10 percent above the national average and 15 percent higher than a decade ago. About half are black or Latino, and they are only a hair's-breadth less likely to earn a bachelor's degree than their classmates.[18] Outside Florida, though, the university still flies under the radar.

Hitt doesn't mind the anonymity. "We're the best university nobody has heard of. That gives us license to experiment."[19]

SCALE × EXCELLENCE = IMPACT

Because the University of Central Florida is a new player on the higher education stage, it can test-drive disruptive approaches that an old-school institution would never contemplate. The road to decision at a place like Yale is as rutted as the Conestoga Trail, and the riposte that "we've always done things this way" carries weight there, but UCF is higher education's Tomorrowland.[20]

If a university is determined to take the dropout question seriously, the message must be delivered emphatically and repeatedly from the top, and action has to follow rhetoric. "Deciding on a course of action means being willing to ask uncomfortable questions, listen seriously to the answers, and then act on them," says Hitt. "A lot of universities aren't that interested in the answers, so they don't dig." The president enlisted top administrators, including the finance and operations vice president, in this cause by making their bonuses partly depend on graduation rates, an unheard-of practice in higher education.

"John's style is to make sure everyone shares across-the-board responsibility for success," explains Dale Whittaker, the president's second-in-command, who succeeded him after he retired in 2018.

In the mid-1990s, the university was growing at a rapid clip. Hitt wanted to get ahead of the game. "Scale x Excellence = Impact" was the mantra.

The obvious way to accommodate more students is to construct more classrooms. While new buildings have kept popping up—students quip that UCF stands for Under Construction Forever—the university couldn't build its way to a solution. Florida is among the stingiest states in bankrolling higher education, and it was inconceivable that the lawmakers would pick up the third-of-a-billion-dollar tab to construct the classrooms and labs required to accommodate a mushrooming student population.

Alternatively, the university could recruit out-of-state students, who pay nearly four times as much as Floridians. That's how schools like the University of Oregon, where half the students come from elsewhere, foot the bill. But that option wasn't on the table because it was inconsistent with how the university defines its role, as providing an affordable education for students from the region. UCF takes pride in the fact that *Kiplinger's* cites it as a "best-value" school, where three-quarters of the undergraduates receive financial aid and nearly half graduate debt-free.

Developing an online program to meet the growing demand looked like the best option. "Scale x Excellence"—not only was virtual education a potential money-saver, it would also enable students to earn a bachelor's degree without having to take all their courses in Orlando. Saving money while opening the university to students a hundred miles away had been the rationale for creating satellite campuses, and online education seemed the logical next step.

Depending on virtual learning to solve an educational problem is a tightrope-walk-risky strategy. In the early 2000s, NYU and Cornell burned through tens of millions of dollars when their online courses didn't attract students.[21] But while those schools were looking for a cash cow, UCF had an educational purpose in mind. It envisioned virtual education, delivered at scale, that would capture the attention of the wired generation and deliver an education as good as a student would get in a traditional classroom.

The results have exceeded UCF's most optimistic projections. "Online learning has gone mainstream," Tom Cavanaugh, who runs the program, tells me. Nearly half of credit hours at the university come from virtual classes and more than three-quarters of the students take some classes online. Most undergraduates mix online and classroom courses—only 3 percent graduate with an online bachelor's degree. "They are in Greek life, they are in the rec center," says Dale Whittaker. "Go to the student union and you'll find students, their laptops open, working side by side side on their courses."

The rise and collapse of the much-hyped MOOC, those massive open online courses that were supposed to revolutionize higher education on the cheap, gave this mode of teaching a bad name.[22] But these courses don't look at all like MOOCs. UCF students who take virtual classes email their professors and join chat rooms. Their grades are almost identical to those of students in brick-and-mortar classrooms. "We can deliver personalized learning because of technology at a scale we've never been able to do," says Cavanagh, and the expanded program allowed UCF to add new students even during the Great Recession.

The university has garnered national awards for online education. Rightly so—no other university makes such smart use of virtual learning.

A thousand students sign up for the introductory business administration class every semester, and no classroom on the campus is big enough to contain all of them. Seats fill up quickly, and the number of students cramming the aisles would give a fire marshal hives. Whether out of choice or necessity, many students watch these lectures on their laptops at a time when it's convenient for them. Instant capture, as it's called, is the simplest form of online instruction. Nothing distinguishes the two versions of the course, aside from students' ability to hit the pause button.

This mode of virtual instruction is the exception at UCF, where almost all of the courses have been developed by professors who, working with design experts, are formulating a new pedagogy that fits a distinctive way of teaching. The professors figure out what bells and whistles will keep their course lively as well as informative, and the designers turn those ideas into course material. As a team of outside reviewers concluded, the online program evolved "over decades as a time-intensive, instructionally oriented process, rather than taking short cuts to speed the process of scaling."[23]

The first lesson in creating an online class, archaeologist Amanda Goff tells me, is that you cannot take what's used in a face-to-face class and paste it onto the web. A professor must start from scratch—What do I want my students to learn? What will bring the course to life? How do I find out whether the students understand the material?

Archaeology would seem to be especially hard to teach this way, since it is intrinsically a hands-on endeavor. To understand ancient civilizations, archaeologists dig up pottery shards and bones, looking for telltale signs of age and place; and in the classroom, students may get a chance to handle those objects. "I have to give online students the feeling they're part of the investigation," says Goff, using a lesson on arrowheads to illustrate her point. "Arrowheads differ depending on where and when they were made—some have fluted points, others are triangular, some are scored, and others are plain. The assignment is to figure out the origin of a mystery arrowhead. The students can view the image from different angles, to see whether it's curved and whether the tip has ridges."

"My students appreciate the flexibility," Goff adds. "Being online means they can be a student and have a life where they can afford to cover the rent." During her office hours, she meets her students face to face or on Skype. "For an undergraduate, everything seems urgent. My computer is always open—I hear the dings whenever a message comes in—and I answer all of them by the next day." Goff uses Twitter for course updates and links to articles she finds on the Internet. "The immediacy is appealing to my students. They know what's going on right away and they like the fact that I'm involved in their technology."

Online teaching has obvious downsides. Students study on their own time, which demands self-discipline. And the online experience doesn't provide room for spontaneity, a student's question leading down a promising intellectual path. This built-in limitation of the technology drives Angel Sanchez crazy—"I don't want a web chat, I want a real conversation," he complains—but he is the exception. "When I offer the same class online and face-to-face, the online section fills up first," says Goff, "and my evaluations are a little better in the online class."

After analyzing thousands of these evaluations, the university concluded that the decisive factor was not whether a course was taught online or in a classroom. What mattered most was the power of the personal—even in the virtual world, students want professors who find a way of reaching out to them.[24]

"AMERICA'S PARTNERSHIP UNIVERSITY"

In his 1992 inaugural address, John Hitt stressed that the University of Central Florida would actively seek out partners. A decade later, it trademarked "America's Partnership University" and "America's Leading Partnership University" as its calling card.

This is UCF's modus operandi, and it is hard to find a government agency, corporation, or nonprofit in Orlando with which it doesn't have ties. "John Hitt has led UCF on a meteoric rise to national prominence, while creating partnerships that are producing the most significant transformation of Central Florida's economy since Disney World opened in 1971," Jeb Bush gushed, in an *Orlando Sentinel* op-ed. "In fact, I believe John Hitt and Walt Disney have done more to transform Central Florida into a vibrant, dynamic place than any two people in the region's history."[25]

By the turn of the century, however, the very fact of UCF's success was jeopardizing its commitment to the region. As its reputation grew, top-of-their-class Florida high school students wanted to enroll, and a school that had admitted almost all applicants a decade earlier was rejecting more than half of them. Freshmen came with strong academic credentials—an average SAT of 1316 and a high school GPA above 4.0, second best in the state.[26] UCF was snaring National Merit Scholars and enticing Florida high school seniors in the top 10 percent of their class by automatically admitting them. It invested in amenities like a rock-climbing wall that millennials take into account when they pick a college.

Meanwhile, local students were losing out. More freshmen were coming from Broward County, a well-off and mostly white enclave north of Miami, than Orange County, where the university is located.

John Hitt insisted that something be done to preserve the university's commitment to accessibility. "That's the key. That's how we can face ourselves," he says.

A partner was needed, and the president didn't have to look far to find the right one, for Valencia College was just half an hour away. Sandy Shugart was of the same mind. "If you want to diversify opportunity, it is the way to go."

"Plugging the Leaky Pipeline"—DirectConnect

As Sandy Shugart tells the story, John Hitt scribbled the blueprint for DirectConnect on the back of an envelope.

"In 2003 I said to John: 'We have a real access problem—students from here can't get into UCF anymore.' He was sure I was going to say 'I'm going to start thirty bachelor's programs.'" Five years earlier, Florida had given community colleges the green light to offer bachelor's degrees, and many of them rushed to compete with the universities for students and state funds. "I don't like that model," Shugart told Hitt. "I would rather our students have access to a hundred bachelor's programs immediately."

Florida's community college graduates were already guaranteed a place at a state university, but they might have to move from Miami to the Panhandle, five hundred miles away, to find a school that was willing to admit them. Only about half the students who earned an associate degree enrolled in a university.

Elsewhere, the process of moving from a two-year to a four-year can be as difficult to master as string theory or Go. Recently, participants at a conference of budding community college presidents were asked to go online, checking whether their school's website simplified the task. "It sucks. Our search engine is so bad I had to use Google," one said. Another added that "there's information on here that is out of date. I know it isn't right, but the student would have no idea." A third administrator recounted an all-too-familiar tale—a student was told by her community college adviser that, after receiving her associate degree, she could transfer to the state university as a junior, only to find out that the university wouldn't accept some credits, obliging her to enroll as a sophomore, because a couple of her classes were taken at a different community college. The one administrator who said that "our website is actually pretty good" acknowledged that "there's no information on who you have to contact with questions."[27]

The situation was entirely different in Orlando. "Let's put our transfer process on steroids by guaranteeing that our graduates can go to UCF," Shugart urged. "You can't say to students 'you might get in.' They need the assurance to motivate them."

The Valencia president could propose this idea to his UCF counterpart because of the close relationship between them that had taken shape over the years. "Our friendship is pretty solid," he says. "He can pick up the phone and call me about anything." Dale Whitaker, John Hitt's successor, plays the harmonica in Sandy Shugart's band.[28]

The two leaders perform an Alphonse-and-Gaston routine, each crediting the other for bringing the idea to life. "Sandy is the key guy," Hitt says. "His predecessor was very difficult to work with. We didn't do a damn thing with him while he was there. When Sandy came in, I saw firsthand that he was a different kind of guy. Is it Oprah who says: 'It's how you made me feel'? If I say we're going to do something, we will do it. Sandy is the same kind of guy, if he tells you he is going to do something he will do it."

Hitt immediately agreed with Shugart's proposal, and when the two men met a week later, he had sketched the model for DirectConnect. There would be a heavy emphasis on advising Valencia students, so that the handoff to UCF was as smooth as possible. Some university courses would be offered on Valencia's campuses, and faculty and facilities would be shared.

Although Valencia was the university's main partner, the graduates of other community colleges in the area would also be guaranteed a place. "Sandy and I have had many conversations about thinking regionally, not parochially," Hitt explains, "and we need a regional education ecosystem."

Nationwide, four in ten college freshmen, including most new-gen students, start out at a community college. But while 80 percent say they want to pursue a bachelor's degree, only 11 percent make it to the finish line. This is the leaky pipeline that DirectConnect is designed to plug.[29] The first joint venture of its kind, the Valencia-UCF compact has been a game-changer for both schools, prompting other universities, including Arizona State, the nation's biggest, to adopt a similar strategy.[30]

DirectConnect has turned into Valencia's most potent weapon to attract students. Highway billboards boast of the link: "Start Here . . . Finish Here." High school graduates from elsewhere in the state, lured by the "2 + 2" guarantee, have flocked to the college. Since the program was launched in 2006, the number of Valencia students earning associate degrees has more than doubled.

The impact on the University of Central Florida has been just as consequential. Since the agreement was inked, more than forty thousand students have enrolled via the transfer route. Half of the university's bachelor's degrees are now being awarded to students who started at a community college. And because most of Valencia's students are black or Latino, DirectConnect has diversified the university's population. Now, nearly half of the university's students are African American or Latino.

Most of these transfer students would have been rejected if they had applied straight out of high school, and when DirectConnect was introduced, critics at UCF complained that the arrangement would weaken the university by introducing less able students. In fact, these students are earning bachelor's degrees at nearly the same rate as their classmates who have been there since their freshman year.

John Hitt attributes this accomplishment to their resilience. "Many of our students have lived tough lives," he says. "They are survivors. They have to be, to get as far as they have."

The partnership is propelling these life-of-hard-knocks students out of poverty and into the middle class. "If you want to increase access to the professions for people of color," says Shugart, "there's only one way to do it—and that's to draw a direct line from transfer to the professions."[31]

Admitting transfers is one thing, making them feel like they fit in is another matter. Both schools are helping the students work through the anticipated academic kinks and personal predicaments. Those efforts begin at the community college, well before the students earn their associate degree. UCF advisers, embedded at Valencia, help prospective transfers stay on track by making sure that the courses they take meet the requirements of their major.

Valencia's satellite campuses have been testing new ways to deepen the DirectConnect model. Kathleen Plinske, president of the campus in Oceola, an hour's drive from Orlando, notes that DirectConnect is the biggest selling point in persuading parents, many of whom didn't graduate from high school, that college is a smart move for their sons and daughters.

"On our campus we developed a program for students interested in majoring in psychology, business, hospitality and tourism, or criminal justice. The students register for a course package with a fixed schedule—say, Tuesday and Thursday afternoons. The intent is that they feel like they are a UCF student from their first day at Valencia." The model is working—after getting their associate degree, many of them head for the university's Orlando campus, because "they want the full college experience."

The number of Oceola undergraduates who earn an associate degree in a STEM field and then pursue a bachelor's degree has ticked up 20 percent in three years. "I wish I could tell you it's a really complex program, but really it's about creating a culture in which everyone believes that students of color can be successful in STEM," Plinske explains. She's echoing one of Valencia's Big Ideas: every student can learn anything under the right conditions.

The hardest task is helping transfer students cross the cultural chasm that separates a nurturing community college like Valencia from a huge university like the University of Central Florida. To go from one place to the other isn't just a trip across town—it's like moving from a village to a metropolis. The coursework is harder at UCF and the expectations higher. Valencia's Dutch-uncle reminders about undone assignments vanish, and many professors, busy with their research, don't go out of their way to bond with their students. For someone accustomed to the give-and-take of small class, courses with five hundred students can be intimidating.

The phenomenon is called "transfer shock," the queasy-in-the-stomach feeling of not truly belonging at the university, and it likely explains why these students' grades dip during their first term at UCF. Wilfredo Ortiz, who graduated with an A- average in engineering, tells me that the transition was rough. "My first semester was pretty overwhelming, to say the least." Even Angel Sanchez, the poster-child for DirectConnect, had a hard time. But by the second semester, transfer students'grades are on the rise. The upper-level classes that they're taking are smaller, which gives them a chance to know their professors, and they're joining campus organizations that introduce them to kindred spirits. A survey found that, after their first year, the transfers wax as enthusiastic about the university as those who came as freshmen.

This pattern—the jolt of the new, the need to find like-minded classmates, the dawning realization that help is there if you seek it—holds true at any outsized university. But while many schools do next to nothing to help transfers, UCF and Valencia College keep looking for ways to bridge that chasm.

Blurring the Community College–University Boundary

A jointly run campus, located in downtown Orlando, is the latest stage in this collaboration. In some ways, it is akin to a recent venture at Georgia State.[32] There, the university absorbed the local community college, introducing its kitbag of strategies—just-in-time mini-grants, data analytics, and revamped introductory courses—to a twenty-one-thousand-student institution that, when the merger took place in 2016, graduated an atrociously low 6 percent of its students.

"It's real here," says Peter Lyons, dean of the community college. "There's a different culture," and every decision that Lyons makes is aimed at reversing the engrained attitude of defeatism, moving away from "What's wrong with our students?" to "What can we do better?" The hope is that what happened in Orlando, with DirectConnect, can happen in Atlanta—that by putting a bachelor's degree within reach, the no-hoops-to-jump-through guarantee will give the community college students a good reason to graduate, and Georgia State will add upperclassmen who have had a solid college experience.

Though the Orlando venture also binds the community college and the university, it is anything but a rescue operation. Building on past experience, the downtown campus gives the two schools a chance to come up with a new kind of hybrid institution.

The campus brings 7,700 students from UCF and Valencia under one roof, taking courses, living and working together, within walking distance of jobs and internships relevant to their area of study. "Downtown industry clusters provide high-impact experiences for our students," says managing director Mike Kilbride. "Students in the legal studies program, for instance, have access to more than 760 companies associated with the legal profession—ten times more than are located near the main university campus—as well as the courts." Eventually, the campus will offer everything from associate degrees to PhDs, further blurring the boundary between the two-year college and the university.

This newest venture in collaboration is another way of making good on the University of Central Florida's belief that Scale x Excellence = Impact. That could just as well be the slogan of DirectConnect.

5

FOCUS ON FRESHMEN
University of Texas

The University of Texas (UT) had a problem—its undergraduates liked bright-lights, biggish-city Austin so much they didn't want to leave. Or that's the optimistic take on it. Many students were simply struggling to finish their degrees. Barely half of each class was graduating in four years.[1]

Most universities find themselves in the same boat. Only a third of undergraduates at flagship public universities like the University of Texas, and barely a sixth at regional universities, earn a degree in four years.[2] The extra time slows these students' progress toward an advanced degree or a good job. It costs them or their parents as much as $40,000, and at public universities, taxpayers foot part of the tab. With undergraduates lingering, there is also less room for other students to enroll. Most important, the longer it takes students to graduate, the more likely they are to drop out.

At UT, the expectation that students would graduate in four years had never been part of the campus culture. "No one ever told the students that they were members of 'the Class of XX.' The faculty's attitude was, 'I stayed in college forever and I don't know why a student wouldn't want to. It's a lovely place. Why not stay for a fifth year?'" says David Laude, popularly known as the "graduation rate champion."

After a Texas-size donnybrook that pitted Gov. Rick Perry, fixated on cost-cutting, against then-president Bill Powers, a deal emerged in 2013. The Texas Board of Regents approved a tuition increase, gave the university $12 million, and agreed to invest in initiatives to help students succeed. The university had already begun drawing up plans to graduate more students on schedule, but the president raised the stakes by pledging that 70 percent of the Class of 2017 would graduate in four years.

It was a wildly ambitious goal. "While I really had 2020 in mind," Powers recalls, "70 percent by 2017" drove the campaign. UT came close, raising the on-time graduation rate from 51 percent to 66 percent between 2012 and 2017. It nearly hit the 70 percent mark in 2018, which enables the university to enroll more than 1,000 additional freshmen. Even more notable, the gap between the campus-wide four-year graduation rate and the rate for low-income, African American, Latino, and first-generation students has been halved.

Bill Powers led the charge, and his point-person, David Laude, possessed the know-how, the passion, and the tenacity to turn aspiration into fact. Laude's strategy was to focus on freshmen, since research shows that most students who drop out have already left by their sophomore year. UT invested most heavily in the students, mainly new-gen undergraduates, whom the data-crunchers predicted to be the least likely to earn an on-time degree.[3] These efforts were augmented by a low-cost intervention that had an outsized impact, as UT became the first university to administer, campus-wide, the brief "mindset" and "belonging" experiences described in Chapter 1.

Every step that UT took was designed to help these students build relationships with their professors, advisers, and mentors—to give them someone they could turn to in times of classroom stress or personal trauma. Laude realized that "if students aren't feeling connected to the university, that someone cares about them, it doesn't matter how many tutoring hours we offer them. In the long run, that's going to be the thing that makes or breaks them."

"Saving Lives"—Why Diversity Matters

"Schizophrenic": that's how many of the people I met during my stay in Austin described the university. "UT has had a love-hate relationship with itself. On the one hand it believes that it's excellent, but on the other hand it's not so sure about its students," says Laude. The institution wants to be seen as in the same league, academically, as one of the nation's premier public universities—a "dare-to-be-great" university," Powers calls it. "We put $50 million into a new telescope. If you want to be in, you can't have a second-rate astronomy department."

But UT's identity is also molded by the diversity of its undergraduates. Thirty percent are African American or Latino, and a quarter receive federal Pell Grants. Three-quarters of the undergraduates are on the campus because of a state law that guarantees admission to anyone graduating in the top 10 percent of their high school class, whether they come from upscale suburbs, where students can take classes in linear algebra and Mandarin, or down-at-the-heels towns in the Panhandle and the Rio Grande Valley, where many high schools lack physics labs and the textbooks are a generation old.[4] The 10 percent rule obliges the university to accept students who, because of their weak SAT scores, would never get into schools like Berkeley or Michigan. In the *U.S. News* rankings, UT suffers, like Georgia State, for making equity a priority.

"Candidly, right now what is holding us back is the 10 percent rule," contended Bill McRaven, then chancellor of the University of Texas system, at a 2016 legislative hearing, inserting himself into a decades-long political debate. "Ten percent isn't the right criterion for Austin. To make sure the right students are coming to the university, that alone will put us in the position to be a more competitive university."[5] You would be hard-pressed to find many UT faculty or administrators who share this position. "We're saving lives," says Carolyn Connerat, who worked closely with David Laude, weaving a moral dimension into our conversation.

This emphasis on diversity dates to the 1970s, when the law school began using race as an explicit criterion for admission. A generation later, a federal appeals court held the practice unconstitutional, but even as other public institutions were readying themselves for similar courtroom defeats, the Texas lawmakers counterpunched. "Conservative rural legislators realized that their population only ended up being 1 percent of the students being trained by the state," Norma Cantu, a UT law professor and civil rights lawyer, points out. "It's as easy for someone who's a goat rancher to understand that as it is for someone who worked for the University of Texas to get it." These legislators joined forces with Latino representatives from the

Rio Grande Valley, and this unlikely coalition pushed through the 10 percent law. In effect, it was an end-run around the judicial ruling, allowing the university to enroll a wide range of students without having to rely on racial quotas.[6]

Expanding access was only the first, and in many ways the easiest, step. These new-gen students needed lots of extra help if they were going to thrive.

"Every Student Can Get an A"

"To improve student outcomes on this campus, you need someone with academic and research chops who is passionate about the mission," Bill Powers says, and this observation holds true everywhere I visited. It's Tim Renick at Georgia State and Sandy Shugart at Valencia. In Austin, David Laude had that role.

"If you look at the story of my life, the chances that I would be sitting here with you are one in a million," says Laude. "Most professors come from status, affluence, or academic standing. I grew up in the Central Valley [of California], no professionals around me, just football coaches and moms. People learn the truth about themselves, which is that they are what they do."

Although he had been a research wunderkind, publishing seventeen first-authored papers while earning his PhD in lightning-speed three years, Laude realized, a few years after joining UT's College of Natural Sciences faculty, that he was happier in the classroom than the laboratory. At the University of Texas, as elsewhere, freshman chemistry, which Laude teaches, as well as calculus and biology, are "weed-out" courses, where tough grading is intended to limit the number of prospective science majors. At the College of Natural Sciences, half of the students were failing at least one of these classes. Disheartened, they abandoned their hope for a STEM career.

Undergraduates know the score. "My biology teacher was retiring. He didn't really care about anything except his research," Iesha Jackson, a UT senior, tells me. She was understandably bitter at how she was treated. "He said he didn't like teaching non-bio majors, and that this was a weed-out class. There was an overload of information, and you're just forced to retain it. You've got these teachers who are really rude and mean. They don't actually care if you learn or not. All that matters is how many people they can get rid of."

David Laude considered himself a good teacher, and his teaching awards attested to his classroom skills. Why, he asked himself, were so many of his students failing? When he scoured their records, he learned that the students earning D's and F's were overwhelmingly poor youth whose third-rate high schools left them unprepared for college-level science. That's why their SAT scores were two hundred points lower than the rest of the class.

"We flunked half of our students in the freshman year," Laude recalls. "We were failing these students because they were poor. We put students with low SAT scores in pre-calculus, and wouldn't let them take chemistry, biology, or math until they passed. Right off the bat, we were telling them that they didn't belong. Boy! did we hold our African Americans and Hispanics with 900 SATs accountable, in their very first experience.

"I ran the data on one cohort that took pre-calculus. Of the more than 700 students—a quarter of the students in the College—zero graduated in the College. Zero."

Laude realized these students needed more personal attention than they received in a five-hundred-student lecture hall. He designed a course for fifty of them, persuading like-minded colleagues in calculus and biology to join the venture. "The message to the students was 'work hard and do your best, and we won't cut you any slack.'"

What began as a classroom experiment was expanded, in 1999, into a program called TIP (Texas Interdisciplinary Plan) Scholars. "Now we call these students 'scholars,' we make them work hard and then they thrive," says Laude.

"I'm in the TIP program because I went to a shitty high school," one student told me. That's the right attitude, says Laude: "'I know I have been denied what the affluent kids have gotten, and it's about time somebody gave me my own.'"

TIP is designed as a catch-up year for freshmen.[7] The students are assigned to a cadre of like-minded classmates—a "learning community," akin to what we've seen at Georgia State—and, as in the Rutgers-Newark honors program, they are mentored by upperclassmen from similar backgrounds.

Mentoring and learning communities are familiar initiatives. What makes TIP unique is the classroom experience—these students are taking STEM classes designed specifically for them, taught by professors who have adopted David Laude's "everyone-can-get-an-A" approach to teaching. "When you come from a high school in the Texas Panhandle or the Rio Grande Valley and you walk into a chemistry class with 500 students, there are issues of belonging and comfort," says Cassie Burton, a TIP academic adviser. "These are students who are leaving their families and communities for the first time, students with mental health issues, students who are blindsided by having to do anything on their own, students who don't understand the obligations of college, students who have to go home a lot to support the family. It just helps to have someone here who can listen and maybe say 'I know what you are going through,' and root for them to get through it."

"I tried to make a kinder and gentler college by emphasizing the personal," says Laude, and enrollment there doubled in the course of a decade. "We didn't admit more students. We just didn't lose them." Meanwhile, TIP expanded to five hundred students. Most of them stayed in the college and were almost as likely to graduate as their more privileged classmates.

Could Laude duplicate this achievement across the campus?

Bringing Student Success to Scale

In 2012, David Laude moved into the provost's office. His assignment was to meet the "70 percent by 2017" goal, which meant expanding the TIP model across the campus.

Today, the TIP-style initiatives that Laude launched serve two thousand freshmen, a quarter of the class, whom the data-mining deems least likely to graduate in four years. A dozen years earlier, when he first offered a bespoke experience to fifty chemistry students, he had to guesstimate whom he should select, but by the time he took on his new assignment the university was using a statistical model that incorporated everything from high school grades and SAT scores to first-gen status to make this calculation. "We now know that the overwhelming reason students are unlikely to graduate on time is family income. College completion is primarily an economic issue," says Laude.

To secure campus-wide buy-in, Laude had to convince skeptical, sometimes hostile, professors and administrators to embrace a new way of thinking about undergraduate education—if the "everyone deserves an A" philosophy of teaching worked in chemistry, there was no reason it shouldn't also work at the business school.

In making his pitch, Laude could count on Bill Powers's forceful backing. Against the advice of some graybeards, who warned him that curriculum reform was the graveyard of presidents, Powers made revamping undergraduate education his legacy issue. Big-enrollment lecture courses were converted into what are referred to as "flipped classes"—students come to class having already read the basic material online, prepared for problem-solving activities in the classroom. And every undergraduate had to take a seminar that lifted them out of their disciplinary comfort zone, as well as obliging students habituated to a diet of multiple-choice exams to write essays.

Powers didn't miss an opportunity to underscore the benefits of earning a bachelor's degree in four years, and this message brought key administrators on board. "What I was able to do," says Laude, "was to say, 'all of us, we're all going to start working in the same direction' and they all agreed to it."

Like everyone else, professors respond to inducements, and the quality of instruction improved when the university introduced financial incentives, including a $7,500 salary boost, for excellence in the classroom. Instead of ridding themselves of students who didn't catch on immediately, more professors strove to help them. In first-year chemistry, the failure rate was halved; in biology, it shrunk by more than two-thirds; and in statistics, it was reduced by three-fourths. The GPA at UT climbed to its highest level in the history of the institution. The courses didn't get easier, the students didn't get brighter, and the faculty didn't embark on a grade-inflation campaign. What changed was the professors' attitudes toward their students.

TIP's multi-pronged approach had proven itself, and in almost every college it serves as the template for the academic success programs. The particulars vary, however, since undergraduates in different fields butt up against distinctive barriers. Laude believed that, in these matters, the colleges, rather the central administration, knew best. Trust but verify: the "70 percent by 2017" team collected information on how the freshmen in the academic success programs were faring, and prodded colleges with disappointing results into rethinking their approach.[8]

The business school was among the last of the colleges to come on board. The impetus came from African American students, who let the dean know that they felt like outsiders who had no right to be there. "We wanted to make sure they weren't getting lost in the shuffle," says Teppera Holman, who runs the freshman program. "We wanted to provide a community, like other students had, and give them the resources to manage the university."

The campus-wide academic success program has been enormously helpful to new-gen students. In 2017, those students, whom the data scientists prognosticated had only a one-in-three chance of graduating in four years, actually earned on-time degrees at almost twice that rate.

Laude doesn't claim much credit. "I don't think I did anything other than incentivize people to care more."

Turning Improbable Scholars into Campus Leaders

For the five hundred freshmen forecast to be the least likely to graduate, David Laude added another layer of support, the University Leadership Network, generally referred to as ULN. He describes it as his proudest accomplishment.

These students come from poor families, and they receive a $5,000 annual scholarship in addition to their regular financial aid package. Without that aid they would have had to work full time at minimum-wage jobs while trying to keep up with their coursework. "The scholarship made a big difference," Ben Aguilar, an English major, tells me. "My friends who aren't in this program are taking forever to graduate. They're focused on working, to pay the rent, not on school."

"These students, universally, live off campus, far away," says Laude. "They view the university as a commuter school, they work in a local laundromat or restaurant and then they leave after a year. The entire idea is to make them feel like they can walk through any door on campus that they want."

"We started thinking about what would be most meaningful during their time at UT and after graduation," adds Jenny Smith, the program's director. "We want to give them the sense that they're leaders. They don't believe it when they come—they think they're imposters who have no business being here—but that attitude gradually changes.

"ULN students meet every Tuesday evening, in business casual, for something like a Ted talk. It's a professional development program. We have lectures and workshops on leadership during their first year, with topics like 'Financial Leadership' and 'Be A Social Change Agent.' When they're sophomores, we put them in internships in a safe environment on campus, like the environmental health office or the planning department, where they can practice their skills. It's their training year. Our peer mentors catch students who need our help, and quickly. Then we groom them to step out. We tell them they have to be prepared to network, polished and ready to go."

Teresa Charnichart, who grew up in Brownsville, in the Rio Grande Valley, was determined to go to college despite the unrelenting opposition of her parents. "You'll spend your money, you'll come back, and you won't have anything to show for it," her father insisted, and he cried when she left. She has no intention of going back: "It's another world there."

Even as a seven-year-old, Teresa, a student at the business school, had the entrepreneurial bug. "Wouldn't it be great to have a place where you could rent a pair of shoes for a dollar a day," she said to her father, after he explained that he couldn't afford to buy her a second pair, and she drew up a business plan. As a high school junior, she took the nine-hour bus ride to Austin and immediately fell in love with the city. "It's the first place I felt at home," she says, and she turned down a full ride at Texas A&M to go there.

"I came into this as an eighteen-year-old with no knowledge of this world," says Ben Aguilar. "There are nine prisons in Huntsville, my home town. It's where all the executions in Texas happen." For most of his classmates, college wasn't on the agenda, and his high school was so bad the state had stripped it of its accreditation. "When I asked my mom how much she'd saved up for his college education, she said 'zero—I never even thought about your going to college.'"

"At the first ULN meeting," Ben says, "I looked around the room. Most of the students were Latino and black, and I thought, 'they're in the same boat as me. The organization was created for people just like me.'" Teresa had a similar reaction. "The group was great. If anyone had something rough going on, we'd spend time letting the person know that there was a silver lining. The business school is so tough and the other students are so smart, so experienced, and they have networks we don't have. We're holding hands, going through the next steps together."

The $5,000 scholarship made it possible for these students to come to UT, and the internships and "business casual" motivational lectures pointed them in the right direction. "It takes a lot of time—a lot of time!" says Teresa, "but it's worth it. The people I've met made me a strong leader. They helped me keep going, helped me get the right perspective on what matters in life."

The University Leadership Network students in the Class of 2017 graduated at a rate far surpassing the number-crunchers' calculations. Only a quarter of them were predicted to earn an on-time bachelor's degree. In fact, more than double that number graduated in four years and almost all the rest are on track to graduate in five years.

David Laude cares deeply about these students, and he learned how to turn his sentiments into an effective program. "On this campus there are a million people who have lots of enthusiasm for fixing things, but that is just a bunch of heat. The difference between heat and work, thermodynamically, is that heat is movement in chaos, randomly, whereas work is movement all in the same direction. What I was able to do was to say, 'all of us, we're all going to start working in the same direction.'"

BELONGING AND GROWTH MINDSET CHANGE THE LIVES OF MINORITY FRESHMEN

David Laude wasn't the only person on the campus with a plan to improve the fortunes of the most vulnerable undergraduates. In 2012, the year Laude moved into the provost's office, psychologist David Yeager, who as a Stanford graduate student had worked on the breakthrough "mindset" and "belonging" research described in Chapter 1, joined the UT faculty.

That research, as we have seen, shows that a brief online experience at the outset of college can allay the fears of students that they didn't deserve to be at the university and that they weren't smart enough to make it. Learning that they weren't imposters and developing a growth, rather than a fixed, mindset equips them with the psychological tools they need to surmount the setbacks—a disappointing grade, harsh comments on a paper—that come with college life. The impact is greatest for minority students, who are especially vulnerable to these negative stereotypes, and the sea-change in their sense of self alters their academic trajectory.[9]

The seminal "belonging" and "mindset" experiments enrolled only about a hundred undergraduates, and were carried out at an elite private university. It was an open—and critical—question whether similarly positive results could be achieved at a far larger scale. The University of Texas provided the ideal laboratory, and it was there that Yeager and his colleagues conducted a study that enrolled nearly the entire incoming freshman class.[10]

The researchers wanted to know whether, a year after the online experience, the freshmen who had participated in the "belonging" or "mindset" activity were more likely than the control group to have completed a full year's course-load and become sophomores in good standing. The results of this experiment confirmed the earlier findings. As the researchers predicted, this forty-five-minute activity made no difference for white students, but the gap for minority students shrunk by 40 percent.[11]

David Yeager's thinking goes well beyond this online activity, and his ideas permeate the Texas campus. Orientation was recast to promote a sense of belonging, with less attention paid to learning the Longhorn fight songs at orientation, and more time devoted to community-building. The math assessment exam, administered a few days after the freshmen arrive, had been described as a do-or-die activity. Now its importance is downplayed—it's not a test, the cover sheet emphasizes, but simply a way for the university to decide which math course is best for you—because research has shown that this softly-softly approach eases the psychological burden for students who doubt their own ability.[12] And the finger-wagging tone of the email informing students that they are on academic probation has been replaced by a "work harder, you can make it" message.

The Master Teacher

David Yeager emphasizes that the brief interventions aren't meant as a cure-all. What happens in the classroom, the lab, the professors' office, and the student organizations has a far bigger and longer-lasting effect.[13]

Case in point—David Laude.

"When the first class starts, I walk to the middle of the room and say, 'I'm on your side. I'm here to make sure you are successful. If that means getting an A, for premed, that is my job. Introduce yourself to those to the left and right of you because we are a team—we are all responsible for one another.' Right off the bat, that changes students' perception of me." Laude's section actually makes greater demands on the students than the other sections—four exams, weekly quizzes and a final—but the majority of the class earns As and almost no one fails. "The difference is that the students work harder because the environment of the classroom is different. You'll find 400 students, computers open, studying together."[14]

"Thanks for the course," one student emailed Laude. "I learned a lot about life." That is his intention. "Students are adept at test-taking, but their development in terms of integrity and perseverance is undermined by the way we elevate the best of the best. Boy can they do well on task x, but human skills—hard work, integrity—are important. That's what I'm teaching.

" 'Integrity is a muscle,' I tell them. I walked into class one day and saw that the candy machine was broken. After one student stole a bag of chips, others did the same. The next day there were riots with people of color stealing TVs. I told the students who stole the chips that 'the only difference between you and them is that you can pay for what you steal.' "

"Hands down one of the best professors at UT," one student wrote on the "Rate My Professor" website. "He truly cares about all of his students getting an A in his class. I used to suck in chemistry in high school, but Laude really taught the class well and made chemistry easy! Definitely take him!" A classmate pointed out that "Dr. Laude's classes are not 'easy'—they require work because chemistry itself is just a difficult subject. Dr. Laude tries to help the best he can and has a clear-cut way for you to study. If you work hard enough and have some luck on your side, you can get an A." These themes—that Laude is a caring professor who brings a fearsome subject to life—are staples in the students' comments. "Congrats if you have him, because you just won the UT equivalent of the lottery," declared one student, in an all-caps encomium.

What's Next?

As graduation drew closer for the Class of 2017, David Laude's team started drilling down to the individual student level. "It was crucial to get student buy-in. We were asking ourselves, 'What will it take to get this student to graduate?'" Carolyn Connerat recalls. Having come so close, the team was asking itself what more they could do. Are students losing time because they don't know which courses satisfy graduation requirements? Are there enough seats in the gateway courses that students must take for their major? Why wasn't there an uptick in on-time graduation rates among those who, according to the data, were the most likely to earn a degree in four years? These students are mostly well-off, undeterred by the cost of spending another year in Austin. Were they simply taking classes that intrigue them, rather than rushing out the door?

Such questions are no longer Laude's concern. "I've been at it long enough," he says, and in the fall of 2017 he returned to the classroom.

Laude cannot understand why any professor would choose to flunk lots of students, instead of doing everything he can to help them master the subject. "Why would anyone come to work every day and carve out a substantial chunk of their life, which is the teaching piece, and have it be unenjoyable, be crappy? Bad teaching, bad grading, angry students. Why not embrace teaching as one of the extraordinary joys of being an academician?" As the student success champion, he had learned that "culture change comes slowly, but that with concerted effort it comes."

Meanwhile, the university keeps looking for ways to do better. "We're not going to be satisfied with 70 percent," says Rachelle Hernandez, David Laude's successor, tells me. "And it's not just about graduation. We want to make sure students leave here with a good job or grad school lined up. That not only helps them, it also helps their families, their communities."

After nearly a decade on the job, Bill Powers resigned as president in 2015—worn down by constant pressure from the chancellor of the university system and the Board of Regents. His successor, Greg Fenves, is sounding the same themes. In his 2017 State of the University Address, he made "increasing UT's role as an engine of upward mobility so that more students and their families can achieve the American dream" his top priority.[15] While this pledge can be read as boilerplate, Fenves is serious. He recruited Stanford economist Raj Chetty, whose research on universities that channel kids from low- or middle-income families to the top 20 percent of American wage earners has attracted national attention. Chetty is searching for other things UT can do to better the prospects of students from the poorest families. "We're not going to look just at peer institutions," Fenves tells me, "but at those that are making a big difference for students." That's why the university was quick to join Georgia State and Arizona State in forming the University Innovation Alliance.

When I ask David Laude why other universities haven't done as much as UT, he has a straightforward answer—most campus leaders are unwilling to do the necessary hard work.

"I've given talks at lots of schools, I give the ra-ra! about what we've done, they come back, 'love the ra-ra,' and I say, 'what are you going to do?' They always choose the one thing that anybody can do. 'I love that you're putting all your new students in some kind of small group.' I tell them 'you need to drill into data, really understand your students,' and they start walking away."

6

THE PROMISE AND THE MINDSET
Long Beach State

The graduation figures from Long Beach State command attention—a 250 percent increase over the course of a generation, an accomplishment matched by few other schools. This record becomes even more noteworthy when you realize that, during these years, the university enrolled more poor and minority applicants—80 percent of the students are African American or Latino, and nearly half receive federal Pell Grants—many with weaker high school credentials than the earlier generation of students.

The Long Beach Promise—a unique collaboration among the city's educational institutions that extends from preschool through PhD—partly explains what has happened, because the synergy that this joint effort generates makes for a stronger university. Like Rutgers-Newark, Georgia State, and the University of Central Florida, Long Beach State regards itself as an anchor institution whose future is intimately intertwined with the city's.

Within the campus precincts, a pull-out-all-the-stops campaign to put "highly valued degrees" in the hands of more students, powered by a determined provost, had a game-changing impact. The next stage in the university's evolution looks just as ambitious: reinventing the culture of the entire university by making "growth mindset" its guidepost. *We all make mistakes—that's how we learn—a bad grade doesn't mean you aren't smart enough to belong here—we can help you do better.*

"Understanding this could make a difference for 10 percent of our students," President Jane Conoley believes, "and that's a big deal."

THE PROMISE

In the "Leave It to Beaver" 1950s, Long Beach, California, was the picture-perfect suburb, dubbed "Iowa by the Sea" by the locals—shorthand for the Midwesterners who flocked to this riposte to neighboring Los Angeles. This was the height of the Cold War, and the United States was spending lavishly on the military. Defense powered the local economy, as the Long Beach Naval Station and McDonnell Douglas aircraft provided tens of thousands of good jobs.

Fast forward to the early 1990s. With the Cold War fast receding into history, military bases were being closed across the country. The Naval Station was shuttered, and McDonnell Douglas, which had accounted for a quarter of the Long Beach workforce and a third of its payroll, laid off half its employees. Riots followed the Rodney King beating, and National Guardsmen patrolled the streets. The Midwesterners fled and the city became a major port of entry for immigrants from Latin America and Asia. The unemployment rate was among the nation's highest, Asian and Latino gangs warred with each other, and the once-thriving downtown had become a crime-plagued ghost town.[1]

Desperate for a turnaround strategy, city leaders adopted what they called the "three Ts and an R" strategy: tourism, technology, trade, and retail. But they knew that this approach, lifted straight from the urban development playbook, wasn't enough to rescue the city. The local educational institutions, from elementary school through college, had to get better.

In the mid-1990s, Long Beach State University, Long Beach City College, and the public schools started to collaborate. In 2007, they officially joined forces to construct a prekindergarten-to-postgraduate continuum of exemplary education. These linkages have upped the game for each of the partners—synergy works.

Every high school graduate from Long Beach and the surrounding towns is entitled to one year of free tuition at Long Beach City College, and students from the community get preferential admissions treatment at Long Beach State. This is the Long Beach Promise, and it has been the driver of change across the institutional landscape.

Since the initiative was launched, the school district's graduation rate has risen nearly 10 percent, to 85 percent. That's slightly higher than the national average and 15 percent higher than similar cities. Go-to-college nudges, which begin in elementary school, when the youngsters visit the college campuses, are having the intended effect. Three-quarters of the high school graduates enroll in college, 10 percent above the national average. There has been an uptick in the number of full-time community college students, which portends higher graduation rates, and more graduates are heading for the university.

Examples of the partnership's work blossom everywhere. University and community college faculty came together to design the preschool curriculum. The public schools are collaborating with the university to make sure its graduates can handle the workload. The community college now relies on high school grades, rather than placement tests, to assign students to math and English classes. This shift represents a vote of confidence in the rigor of public school teaching, a rarity in higher education. As a result, fewer freshmen have to take dead-end remedial courses. And Long Beach State professors are working with their community college colleagues to increase the number of students who continue their education at the university.[2]

The headline news comes from Long Beach State, widely known as "the Beach," where, incredibly, the graduation rate increased *two-and-a-half times*, from 26 percent in 1999 to 67 percent in 2017. The university has turned into a go-to school. With nearly 100,000 applicants, the seventh-highest number nationwide, it could admit a class composed entirely of students with 24-karat credentials. Instead, it accepts local students with substantially weaker grades and SAT scores. Those students are likelier to graduate than their classmates from outside the region.

The Long Beach model has garnered its share of national attention, with glowing reports in the *New York Times* and *The Atlantic*, but no other community has been able to copy it.[3] Elsewhere, high schools and universities operate in silos—the former concentrate on getting more students to earn diplomas, not tracking their performance after they graduate, while the latter pay scant attention to what goes on in the local schools. When a university is chastised for its abysmal graduation rate, the reflexive response is to blame the schools and toughen admissions requirements. But at Long Beach State, like Georgia State, Rutgers-Newark, and the University of Central Florida, the attitude is very different—we do the best we can to educate the students we have.

"We don't want to be Harvard," Provost Brian Jersky tells me, "and we couldn't be Harvard, even if we only admitted the top people. And Harvard can't be us. We don't want to play in that pool—we can't. We want to be the best in our pool, and we think we are." In a recent study of universities that operate as engines of social mobility, Long Beach State ranked among the nation's best in moving students from poverty into the middle class.[4]

Four times a year, the heads of the school district, community college and university, joined by the mayor, get together. Mayor Robert Garcia, a product of the local schools, with a doctorate from the university, was at the spring 2017 meeting I attended. So was long-time school superintendent Chris Steinhauser, another Long Beach lifer; Jane Conoley, the president of Long Beach State; and the acting president of Long Beach City College, Ann-Marie Gabel.

"The Long Beach Promise gives us an edge," Eloy Oakley, the former president of Long Beach City College observes. From his current post as chancellor of the 114 college community-college system, he is on top of what's happening elsewhere. "For a decade, the same people were running the three institutions. Two of them left in recent years, but the system hasn't missed a beat. The infrastructure can withstand changes in leadership."

There's no facilitator at this meeting, no formal agenda and no one keeping track of time. "We're planning to phase out remedial math," Jane Conoley informed her colleagues, a change, mandated by the state, that will affect the city's other institutions. Chris Steinhauser reported that a dashboard tracking a student's progress from public school through college was in place, a technically impressive feat because these data systems don't readily mesh with one another. The group tossed out ideas about how the city and state could make higher education more affordable.

Mayor Garcia, a vocal advocate for early education, had pledged in his campaign to make prekindergarten available to every four-year-old. "What do you think about a ballot measure that would bring universal preschool statewide?" he asked. Although this isn't something most campus leaders would take an interest in, these leaders are big backers of the mayor's preschool agenda. "We put up a picture of a preschool student," Eloy Oakley tells me. "Then I ask myself, 'What are we going to do today to ensure that in 2027 this student will be on the platform graduating.'"

Jane Conoley, who arrived in 2015, was still learning on the job. She was not reluctant to ask the kind of "help me understand" questions that, in a more status-conscious setting, would be perceived as a sign of weakness. "The Long Beach Promise was a big draw," she says, explaining why the president's job was so appealing. She had been a dean at the University of California at Santa Barbara, which ranks among the top thirty universities worldwide.[5] "It's a great university, but professors at those institutions are mainly committed to research. While research is important here, there's a stronger commitment to our students. Making sure they graduate is everyone's business."

What *didn't* happen at this meeting is as noteworthy as what was discussed—no one said, "That's not my problem." As Chris Steinhauser notes, "We park our egos at the door." These signals from the top filter down, and across the systems the managers are working closely together.

"We've built a working culture, where everyone feels safe talking about failures, and we're building something together," says Robert Tagorda, who leads the school system's equity initiatives. Not that it's all sweetness and light—"We know that every institution has its own agenda and its own politics. What stops [institutions elsewhere] from partnering is that they're not willing to talk about their own barriers, but we do. We're not trying to bulldoze the bureaucracies, but we've decided that the success of our students across the systems is what really matters."

A deeply rooted sense of place, an abiding pride in the city—I kept hearing these themes during my visit. This can-do attitude explains why, when Jane Conoley asked Chris Steinhauser about 260 high school seniors who barely missed the cutoff for admission, the superintendent reached out to those students, urging them to retake the placement exam. "One hundred twenty-one improved their scores enough to get into the university," Steinhauser recounts. Seventeen of them were African American—particularly good news, since the number of black undergraduates has been declining and the university is anxious to reverse that trend.

Budgets were slashed during the Great Recession, and the public schools were forced to lay off teachers. "Last hired, first fired" was the rule, and as a result, dynamic young teachers lost their jobs. But teachers in special education and STEM, fields where instructors are hard to find, were exempted from that edict. The university stepped in, retooling, at no charge, every Long Beach teacher who wanted to enter one of those fields.

"The Long Beach Miracle" is how a breathless headline writer at *The Atlantic* captioned what is taking place there. But there's no miracle to report, nothing that couldn't be achieved in scores of cities. "What we do is surprisingly simple but amazingly powerful," says Jane Conoley. "We communicate all the time. No turf—just building and evaluating programs, with the goal of removing barriers and supporting student success."

THE "HIGHLY VALUED DEGREE"

Ask campus leaders why the dropout rate plummeted, and everyone proffers the same explanation—Dave Dowell, the former provost, made it happen.

Dowell was unfailingly courteous, a patient listener, unflappable in the face of disputatiousness. Even those who disagreed with him prefaced their remarks by saying: "I liked Dave, but . . ." Yet there was no mistaking the force and singlemindedness of his commitment to undergraduates, no doubting his adroitness in keeping the graduation rate at the top of the university's agenda for more than a decade.

Dowell's epiphany came in 2005, when he visited Elizabeth City State University, a historically black North Carolina college. Although students there had bottom-of-the-barrel high school grades and SAT scores, they were nearly as likely to earn bachelor's degrees as the infinitely better-prepared Long Beach State undergraduates. "That visit was a career-changer," Dowell told a campus magazine. "I realized that the common but unexamined assumption in higher education—that student outcomes depend entirely on the student—is false. There is much that an institution can do to support the success of students. The rest of my career was spent working out the implications of this realization."[6]

The "highly valued degree initiative" is how Dowell branded a university-wide drive to boost the graduation rate and shrink the gap for new-gen students. Assuring that students receive a rigorous education and getting them across the finish line underlay his decisions. "He wasn't just about the numbers," his wife, Nancy Manriquez Dowell, tells me. "He came out of a civil rights background and he knew that every student had a story. He was always rooting for the underdog—the English learners, the economically disadvantaged, students with different life experiences."

Anna Statheros-Anderson picked Long Beach State "because of the environment, the professors, the students, the culture there. So far it's been a great experience, a supportive environment."

"The academic requirements demand a lot of time. What becomes a bigger challenge is life that happens on top of trying not to fall behind. I'm not sure what the answer is. I'm fifty, I'm a mom, I'm responsible, I'm highly motivated. I want to get my bachelor's at least, ideally my master's.

"The counseling office helped so that I could manage my own personal challenges and my challenges outside of school. The counselor was great. I was panicking, what am I doing with psychology? I've been in accounting for years, it makes me money, I thought, I should major in business. When I met with the counselor, I was telling her my woes and my regrets, she said, 'There are so many people with psych degrees, you can use it in business, you don't have to have a business degree unless you're a CPA or something similar,' which I don't want to do. If I hadn't talked to her, I'd still be stewing about changing my major. Business classes aren't where my heart is. You have to have guidance—being able to talk to my counselor, lay it out, say the words out of your mouth, makes you come to terms with what doesn't sound good or right."

Money talks, and the provost deployed his control over the budget as a bludgeon to accomplish this objective. "Managing to impact" was his favorite phrase—there would be no "magpie-ism," no boutique programs that lavished resources on a handful of students. Earlier, some undergraduates had been forced to wait a year or more to take courses required for their major, which stalled their progress to a degree. The bottlenecks were eliminated, as departments were obliged to expand enrollment in those classes to meet student demand.

"Conversations always focused on metrics," Lynn Mahoney, Dowell's comrade-in-arms during those years, tells me. "Each college and department had a six-year graduation goal, and if they fell short, Dave wanted to know why. If a dean or a professor wanted to do anything that cost money, they had to back up their request with data. 'You are full of new ideas,' Dave would say. 'How will your new idea affect graduation rates?'"

"Everyone's job, including the groundskeepers and the campus police, was to do whatever they could to get people to graduate," says King Alexander, the Long Beach State president during this era. "When we hired a dean, we asked: 'What role does your college have in the K–12 pipeline? Were you involved with the public schools in your previous job?' If the answer was 'It's us-versus-them,' they didn't get the job. People on campus spoke about '*our* student success mission,' and students laughed about the fact that the dining hall napkins were imprinted with the message that 'Graduation begins today.' When students hit a certain number of units, they'd get an email saying 'Graduation begins tomorrow,' and if they missed the mark, the message was 'Graduation should have happened yesterday.'"

Traditionalists among the faculty were aghast. To their way of thinking, the "high-value degree initiative" was nothing more than a "high-velocity degree initiative," a way to push students out the door. Dowell was unfazed. "Pushing back on Dave was like pushing back on a noodle," Lynn Mahoney says. "He'd listen calmly, nodding 'no.'"

As the provost saw it, these new-gen students, unsure whether they ought to be in college, required dollops of personal attention. At the apogee of the Great Recession, when other campus initiatives were being cut, he made the same decision as Mark Becker at Georgia State, hiring a cadre of advisers to help students find their way through the academic maze.

Many professors complained that this money should have been used to appoint more of their kind. "We can do the advising ourselves," they contended, but Dowell was unconvinced. As he saw it, when professors took on that responsibility they usually did a slapdash job, for while they knew their department and their discipline, they weren't familiar with how the rest of the university operated. The students, he believed, deserved better than that. (This decision to hire advisers still rankles. "I was recently cornered by five professors, each of whom told me that student affairs has no place on campus and that we're taking seats away from the faculty," Charity Bowles, director of student affairs, told me.)

Eliminating bottleneck classes, reaching out to students, adding advisers, pushing deans to meet graduation goals, designing pathways to graduation—none of this is break-the-mold stuff. Combining these strategies is what made the difference. Dowell concentrated on fixing what he called the unsexy stuff, "what goes on beneath the water line." At his retirement dinner, a graph that charted the increase in the percentage of students who received bachelors' degrees was wheeled out. "Here's what I'm proudest of," he told the gathering, pointing not to a period of rapid improvement but to a time when the graduation rate was flat. Those were the recession years, when lawmakers shredded California's higher education budget, he explained, and "we didn't lose ground."

The Virtues of Pragmatism

Dave Dowell's approach—do whatever it takes to meet students' needs—yielded outsized results. But while administrators come and go, tenured faculty stay forever. Was it wiser to go boldly and quickly or patiently build a consensus for change? On this essential point, the provost and the president disagreed.

Dowell died in 2016, shortly after retiring. Brian Jersky, Dowell's successor, who describes himself as a "pragmatist," is in the president's camp. Although the new provost has restored some of the deans' authority, he has not ushered in a return to the era when the deans ran their colleges like baronies. Like David Laude at Texas, Jersky has given them considerable latitude over their budgets while holding them accountable for metric-driven results.

The student advising system illustrates this philosophy of leadership. At present, each college determines how much money should be spent on advising, and as a result, advisers at some colleges are responsible for more than a thousand students. Jersky favors Georgia State's approach of bringing most academic advisers under one roof, where they can receive the same training and coaching. But the pragmatist appreciates that moving abruptly in that direction would lead the deans to mutiny, and so he is taking a one-step-at-a-time approach. To get a handle on the situation, he asked the deans to supply basic information about the number of students the advisers are seeing. If, as anticipated, the data shows that the system is faltering, he will have the ammunition to reform it. In any event, greater accountability is coming. The California State Regents, the system's governing board, decided that state dollars should be tied to standards that include improving the caliber of advising and raising four-year graduation rates, which strengthens Jersky's hand.

Dave Dowell gave a short, sharp—and needed—shock to a university that had grown complacent. Different times, different circumstances—relying on continuous and measurable improvement makes better sense now.

Experiments in Mindset and Belonging

Across the campus, a hardy band of professors, working in tandem with Jane Conoley, is incorporating the concepts of "mindset" and "belonging" in their courses. No other university is doing as much.

As the experience at the University of Texas attests, a brief online activity during the first days of college, when students are feeling especially vulnerable, can have an outsized impact. But the psychologists who constructed and field-tested these experiences are the first to tell you that encouraging students to adopt a growth mindset and showing them that they are not imposters aren't one-off solutions to the dropout problem. The lives of students can be viewed through this psychological prism—how they are treated at the bursar's office, or how the letter informing students that they are on probation is worded, or how a professor responds when her students are flailing, whether "it's my job to teach, your job to learn" or "we're in this together."[7]

Students need to understand why what's being taught is relevant to them—not "I'm taking a writing class because I have to," but "I'm taking a writing class because it gives me a valuable skill." They need faculty who can push them to think, not parrot a lecture on an exam. And they need to know that their professors are in their corner—that they are coaches, not judges—which is why they are being pushed to keep at it and helped over the hurdles. In short, learning is most likely to take place when there's a challenging curriculum, a talented teacher, and an engaged student. This is why, as we've witnessed, CUNY Start records such glowing results in teaching the basics to freshmen who are years behind their classmates; why, at the University of Texas, David Laude's chemistry students earn As; and why three times more students pass Statway, which takes them from middle-school math through college-level statistics in a single year, than old-school remedial math.[8]

Most university professors have never had a day's worth of training in how to teach. Some possess an instinctive grasp of what works, and they're likely to keep honing their skills; others are skeptical, if not downright hostile, about the mindset insights. "You're just pampering students," some contend, while others insist, against all the evidence, that this is how they teach already.

Enter Kris Slowinski, the Johnny Appleseed of the growth mindset way of teaching at Long Beach State. A poster that asks "What Kind of Mindset Do You Have?" hangs on the door of his cramped office in the chemistry department, where books and papers pile up, and Peet's coffee cups tumble out of the waste paper basket. Although he has an arm's-length-long list of publications and six-figure grants to his credit, his focus these days is on bettering the quality of teaching. As an academic dean, Slowinski spends much of his time persuading his colleagues at the College of Natural Sciences and Mathematics—and, more broadly, across the university—to think "mindset."

Slowinski was frustrated by the number of students who migrated away from chemistry. Like David Laude at UT, motivated by the sheer number of students who failed basic science and math classes, he wanted to reverse the trend. But while Laude relied on his own experience as a professor to decide what mode of teaching was most effective, Slowinski embraced growth-mindset thinking. "This is exactly what our students need," he concluded, after hearing a speech that laid out the model. Together with a colleague, he designed a class in "science success" for nearly four hundred prospective science and math majors.

After watching a video on neuroplasticity—"the brain is a muscle," a growth-mindset staple, is the theme—students in Slowinski's freshman course write about how the concept influenced their thinking. "I have already encountered some academic challenges," one student wrote. "I've received two bad chemistry grades and it had really discouraged me. Now I have decided that rather than give up, which would jeopardize my plans for the future, I'll work harder. I've been to my professor's office hours and am looking into tutoring. I am not letting my bad grades keep me from overcoming this obstacle and am pushing to try harder." A classmate describes how he was shocked when he failed his first exam, the first time he ever received a failing grade. "I didn't spend a lot of time preparing because I thought I knew the material. I try not to be too hard on myself—everyone says many people don't do well on the first test because they don't know what to expect from their professors. This test was a lesson, which has taught me to study the material longer even if I think I know."

Andrea Johnson, who teaches a freshman pre-calculus course, explains how she gets the concept of growth mindset across. "The first time I tried this, I gave the students a survey and all of them knew how to answer—they all had growth mindsets already. But then I gave them a tough problem and they gave up in ten seconds." Now she sets a problem for them to solve and watches how they react. "I show them images of oddly shaped vessels of water and ask them to sketch what the surface of the water would look like from the top and from the side. The students have never been asked to do this before, and I tracked how long it took before people gave up. Afterward, we discussed how long you sit there staring before giving up or seeking help. I don't want to rob them of the chance to be confused for a little bit. Then I ask them to try something they know is wrong. It unlocks the door for them to think about what's wrong. Then they work in pairs, comparing notes, and then in small groups, and finally reaching consensus as a class. They get the idea—you're not born able to draw this object, but if you believe you can learn something, with time and effort you can do it."

In the Science and Math Center, down the hall from Slowinski's office, students are working on their laptops, immersed in their textbooks, talking to one another or discussing a problem with one of the tutors. "They're here when I arrive, and the place is full of students at seven o'clock, when I leave," says Valerie Bagley, who coordinates the program. "The students are all debating, trying to help each other."

Michael Carrillo, one of the tutors, is cut out for the job. He's brainy and personable, someone any student who's stumped by an assignment could readily relate to. In elementary school, he became captivated by science because it offered an escape from the chaotic world in which he was growing up. "Science gave me a new way of looking at things, and you could create things that could make a difference. I walk in the door and write my name in big letters on the whiteboard that says, 'I'm Here to Help You.' "

These students are taking biochemistry and organic chemistry, two killer courses that STEM departments typically use to discourage students with less-than-stellar science backgrounds from continuing in the field. "We want to reassure them that they are headed in the right direction and motivate those who aren't enthusiastic," says Bagley.

"We love the word *yet*.—'I'm just not good at biochemistry' versus 'I'm just not good at biochemistry . . . *yet*.' The students turn it into a joke, but they get the point."

Perseverance isn't just a slogan in this lab. "We're not afraid to hire students who failed a class, as long as they came back and did well the second time."

While the Science and Math Center is a boon for the students, Slowinski knows that, if the message of mindset and belonging is going to be amplified, his colleagues must revamp their courses. "The idea is to expose freshmen to this material in different places, from different angles," he tells me, and that can only happen if enough professors sign on. A day-long workshop drew twenty-five STEM faculty, many of them new to teaching and eager to test a promising pedagogy in their classrooms. Word spread, and there were more takers the second time the workshop was offered.

"This is not a concept that is easy for faculty to absorb," Slowinski says. Although almost everyone who came to the workshop reported that it was useful, a single dose of training cannot do the trick—it is hard to shake old habits, even for fired-up teachers. "The faculty emphasize success, the end of the road, and not the process of getting there. No matter how willing they are, they need to rethink everything they think they know about teaching."

Some members of the department dismiss the benefits of mindset-infused teaching. "There's a culture clash between philosophies," says Andrea Johnson. "I have higher passing rates than my colleagues. Although we wrote the exam together, some of them believe that I am not being stringent if my passing rate is high and they hound me for that: 'I'm wary if anyone has a passing rate that's higher than 70 percent.'"

True to his calling as a scientist, Slowinski is testing several models. "We are carrying out a psychological survey to see which interventions work for which kinds of students." One experiment looks at whether experiences designed specifically for undergraduates who are unsure whether they're cut out for the university will have an impact. Another compares the effectiveness of an intervention emphasizing the plasticity of the brain with another that focuses on the concept of mindset. "This isn't Stanford, where everyone is at the same level. We have students in the same class from entirely different academic backgrounds. One student does a calculation five times faster than her friend. 'Is she smarter than I am?' the student wonders. Once you get students to understand that this difference isn't due to inherent ability but to practice, their attitude changes completely."

Launching a Campus-Wide Mindset Movement

Elsewhere on the campus, other professors have been looking for ways of teaching that work especially well with new-gen students. At the College of Engineering, Dean Forouzan Golshani tells me, while the college was awarding more degrees, minority students were leaving in droves. "Since the time I spent in Ghana, in the late 1970s, I've been concerned about equity. I'm involved with Baha'i students in Iran, who have been denied a postsecondary education. The real problem for all of these kids is lack of opportunity."

In the fall of 2014, Golshani devised a program for twenty-five freshmen who looked like lost causes. Not a single student with the same high school record had ever earned an engineering degree at Long Beach State. Golshani was unconvinced that failure was inevitable. He had these students—like their counterparts in the TIP program at the University of Texas—take their classes together. The courses incorporated a heavy dose of hands-on activity and just-in-time help from tutors and advisers. After that year, the students were left on their own.

The dean couldn't believe the results. All but three of these students completed the introductory calculus and physics courses, most with Bs and better, and almost all of them went on to earn an engineering degree. "One guy had a 4.0 GPA," Golshani marveled. "Remember that he was supposed to fail and leave! We're planning to enroll 100 students and that will close the opportunity gap."

Jane Conoley's dream is to make "mindset" the Long Beach State University calling card. Is that a realistic ambition at a large, financially strapped public university?

"Telling professors 'you need to read this book' is the surest way to kill an idea," she jokes, yet that's more or less what she told the deans. The book was *Mindset*. "I never had a president ask me to read a book and talk about it," exclaims one of those administrators.

Conoley places more faith in the efficacy of the mindset philosophy, and is more committed to embedding it campus-wide, than any university leader I've encountered. As a psychologist whose research on student achievement introduced her to Carol Dweck's work, she comes by her enthusiasm naturally. (Her husband, a UC-Santa Barbara psychology professor, is collaborating with Kris Slowinsky on the mindset experiments.) The simple fact of her commitment gives mindset a certain cachet.

"Can we bring these strategies to scale?" the president asked her colleagues, and they were optimistic. Already, change is afoot. At freshman orientation, students complete an online exercise similar to what's used at the University of Texas. Instead of having to endure a tedious recital of do's-and-don'ts, the newcomers learn from upperclassmen how they handled the sometimes-rocky first months. Student disciplinary hearings have adopted a restorative justice, learn-from-your-mistakes approach. The bursar's office has become more user-friendly, helping students find ways to pay their tuition bill rather than dunning them. And students placed on probation are told that this isn't a signal to leave but a wake-up call.

Trying to remake the culture of a campus is not an assignment for the faint of heart. When a proposal impinges on what professors claim as their turf, argues Conoley, "that change must come organically, it must come from the faculty." She doesn't have much choice, since she presides over a campus where the deans are a force to be reckoned with and the faculty union is antagonistic toward innovations proposed by the leadership. The Academic Senate holds considerable influence, and its chair, English professor Norbert Schurer, dismisses mindset as a fad. Professors have been teaching this way for years, he insists, and now the scientists, having just come upon the idea, are making a needless fuss. (Schurer also scoffs at the potential for technological innovation: "The quill pen is technology.")

Conoley is relying on what she calls "the coalition of the willing" to make the case, anticipating that a critical mass of professors will ultimately sign on. Meanwhile, she is using the incentives at her disposal—money and release-from-teaching time—to nurture initiatives that make courses more mindset-oriented. Money is a hen's-teeth-scarce commodity at this university, where, as at the other twenty-three Cal State campuses, state funds have been cut 20 percent in the last decade, and so small sums and time to do research are powerful motivators. The president is also counting on the next generation of professors to take up the cause, and so she has redesigned the orientation for new faculty to include a discussion of mindset-infused pedagogy.

"This is a good start," Kris Slowinski tells me, "but what's necessary is a campus-wide effort to show faculty, staff, administrators, and students what it *means* to have a growth mindset. That will require numerous workshops, slogans like 'Learn through mistakes' and 'Effort leads to successes' plastered across the campus, maybe even incorporating those concepts in the university's statement of its mission. For change to happen, there needs to be a university culture of fostering growth-minded behaviors." If this kind of change is going to come about at any university, Long Beach State will be the place.

"BELONGING" AT AN ELITE INSTITUTION
Amherst College

What does a small, gilt-edged private college like Amherst have in common with a big public university like the University of Central Florida or Georgia State? Next to nothing, to judge from appearances. But dig deeper, and these schools have a common task—showing their students that they are rightfully there, at a school that values their presence.

Universities like Long Beach State and community colleges like Valencia are forever finding new ways to evoke a sense of belonging among their students, in order to increase the likelihood that their students will graduate. Dropping out doesn't figure into the equation at schools like Amherst College, where 95 percent of the students graduate. But as Harvard sociologist Tony Jack, himself an Amherst alumnus, points out to me, "Academic life is inherently social. Focusing solely on grades or graduation rates obscures that fact." Every school, regardless of whether it admits all comers, like the CUNY community colleges, or is highly selective, like Amherst, must figure out how to empower its students. If it fails, first-gen students—sensing that they are seen as marginal figures admitted out of a mistaken sense of noblesse oblige, not as citizens whose voices count—will do what they feel is necessary to make themselves visible.

Across the landscape of higher education, the demand to be treated by the institution as full members has been vigorously pressed, especially by African American and Latino students. Campuses across the country were convulsed by the failure of the University of Missouri to respond forcefully to acts of bigotry. At Yale and Princeton, demonstrations were sparked by outrage that the campus honored a slave trader, in the first instance, and a president who held racist views, in the second.

At Amherst College, students launched a campus-wide protest that came to be known as the Amherst Uprising. Attention must be paid—this event prompted the college to think deeply about how to construct a community where diversity is an asset, a community in which everyone, new-gen and old-gen alike, can experience a genuine sense of ownership.

The Amherst Uprising

The protest began quietly enough on November 11, 2015, with a message posted on Facebook urging students to join a one-hour sit-in at the Robert Frost Library, at the heart of the campus, "stand[ing] in solidarity with the students in Mizzou, Yale, South Africa, and every other institution across the world where black people are marginalized and threatened."[1]

The day was clear and unseasonably warm, the temperature climbing into the seventies, and as word of the demonstration spread, hundreds of students, as well as faculty and staff, crowded into the library. Initially, students spoke about what was happening elsewhere, but the focus quickly shifted to their own lives. They testified about the wounds of race and class that they, personally, had suffered—stories that few of the white students had heard—and bared their feelings of alienation and invisibility.

"All of a sudden people started sharing stories about their experiences with racism on campus," recalls Alida Mitau. "Having a white student start touching a black student's hair, that was particularly bad. An African American student, an athlete, talked about how none of his teammates listened to him. More and more people started sitting down and listening. People were crying."

"I had some close friends who went up and spoke," says Danny Cox. "I was surprised by how frequently they said that they dealt with challenges and oppression, how hurtful it had been to them. The number of people who could go up there and tell these stories was surprising and enlightening."

President Biddy Martin, who was about to board a flight to Japan, canceled her trip and rushed back to campus. In the heat of the moment, fifty self-styled leaders of the protest presented the president with a list of demands—get rid of the unofficial school mascot, Lord Jeff, the sobriquet for Jeffery Amherst, best known for advocating that smallpox-infected blankets be given to the "disaffected" Native American tribes; tear down posters that read "In memoriam of free speech, the true victim of the Missouri protests"; and require that the students who displayed them undergo racial sensitivity training. The activists wanted the president and the trustees to apologize for "our institutional legacy of white supremacy," among many forms of discrimination, including "heterosexism, cis-sexism, xenophobia, anti-Semitism, ableism, mental health stigma, and classism."

As the sit-in continued through the weekend, attracting much of the college community, who stopped by to see what was happening and remained to listen, its leaders rethought their strategy. "We made the list of demands in haste, with urgency and emotion," they explained. What was needed, they realized, wasn't an ultimatum but a long-haul campus-wide effort to "to bring about structural and social change."

"Over the course of several days, a significant number of students have spoken eloquently and movingly about their experiences of racism and prejudice," Biddy Martin told the campus. "The depth and intensity of their pain and exhaustion are evident. That pain is real. Their expressions of loneliness and sense of invisibility are heartrending. No attempt to minimize or trivialize those feelings will be convincing to those of us who listened."[2]

The ferocity of the protest, the powerful and painful recollections that surfaced, took many by surprise. In recent years, Amherst has recast itself as the avatar of racial and socioeconomic inclusiveness. The protestors' message was plain—the college had to do a lot more than change the composition of its student body to become a community in more than the college-catalog sense.

"The protest was a gift," Biddy Martin tells me. "We could make the point to trustees and faculty that these issues are real." Her promise that Amherst would take the students' plaints and proposals seriously has been borne out, as the school has redoubled its efforts to become genuinely inclusive. While the project of inclusion remains a work in progress—advancing inclusion will *always* be a work in progress—the institution has much to show for its efforts.

The Persisting Power of the Past

What happened at Amherst is not simply a story about the travails of a small New England college. Every top-of-the-pecking-order school that aspires to become more racially and economically diverse—and they all pay at least lip service to that aspiration—will encounter similar, if less dramatically presented, tests of its values and practices. The essential question is this— *How does a school like Amherst, with resources beyond the dreams of the schools we've been looking at, foster a sense of belonging among its new-gen students?*

History matters at a tradition-drenched school like Amherst College. You can trace its commitment to the idea of inclusion to its 1821 founding mission—to educate, free of charge, "indigent young men of promising talents and hopeful piety."[3] But for much of its history, Amherst trained mostly well-heeled and prep-school-educated young men, many of them the sons and grandsons of alumni, and almost all of them white, to assume their self-appointed place as masters of the universe. The education was cold-shower rigorous. The beau ideal was the "whole man," who was at once a scholar, an athlete, and a leader. "Privilege is here," as President John F. Kennedy observed, in a speech, delivered weeks before his assassination, dedicating the Frost Library.[4]

Amherst came late to the cause of racial justice. While archrival Williams College was avidly pursuing black applicants, Amherst held back, and until the late 1960s, only a handful of black students were enrolled in each class. The first expression of anger on the campus came in 1970, when 250 students from Amherst and its neighboring colleges staged a sit-in to protest racial tokenism. The dean of admissions was unmoved. "Does the faculty wish to alter its academic pace and admit fewer qualified students?" he asked, a rhetorical question that infuriated the students, and within a few years the number of minority students grew exponentially.[5]

The college's 1974 decision to admit women marked a consequential and controversial transformation. Supporters and opponents debated matters of principle and pedagogy—Could men concentrate on academics with women in the classroom? Could women be themselves in a co-ed environment?—but little thought was given to the practical implications of going co-ed. Every aspect of college life should have been on the table—faculty and staff hiring, courses, athletics, fraternities, codes of conduct—but the only concrete plan was to redesign the dormitory bathrooms.

Act now, address the fallout later—that is also how Amherst College treated socioeconomic diversity. "When we went coed, we hadn't thought a lot about it," recalls political scientist Austin Sarat, "and when we decided to diversify, we replicated that problem."

The drive to create a more variegated Amherst began in earnest in the early 1980s, as the number of minority students steadily mounted. But the college stumbled a few years later, when it admitted a cluster of first-generation, high-need students. "We were an experiment," saya Rick Lopez, dean of new students, who was one of those students. "We loved our education, but it was alienating. We couldn't afford freshman orientation activities that cost money and there was no way for students on financial aid to join clubs." Political science professor Kristen Bumiller views the "experiment" through the other end of the lens. "The prevailing ethos was Dickensian: 'let in the poor wretches.'"

Tom Gerety, who became president in 1994, quickly discovered that "our effort in enrolling poor students and students of color was slapdash, based on a kind of merry, easygoing whimsy. We were coasting along without any discipline or rigor, and we weren't pulling in a more varied and impressive class. I knew what I wanted—limits on legacies and athletics, no favorite schools, outreach to poorer places around the country, stronger results in both diversity and intellectual drive, and not least, strong analysis of our efforts and our results."

You can date the shift—away from being a school that cared about socio-economic diversity in a casual and unfocused way to becoming the nation's poster-child for inclusion at elite colleges—to the hiring, in 1999, of Tom Parker as director of admissions and financial aid. With strong backing from Tom Gerety and his successor, Tony Marx, Parker engineered a quiet revolution.

Parker had been a first-gen student at Williams College in the 1960s, the poor kid from Brooklyn among the preppies, who could afford to go there only because he had a full financial ride. "I'd constantly be reminded of my status. My classmates did not believe I couldn't pay for anything I wanted. My roommate would buy stuff, wait till a check bounced, then call his father to put more money in the bank. I worked overtime in a liquor store,

Christmas Day and New Year's Eve, for pocket money." Decades later, when he returned to Williams as an admissions officer, "I had my cause— dramatically increase the number of kids on aid, first-generation students, and students of color. We reached out nationwide to promising kids from poor backgrounds."

The Williams alumni raised hell when they saw that their sons and daughters were having a harder time getting admitted. "I was called a moron, a fucking asshole who was spreading the diversity plague." But Parker got results, as the number of students on financial aid grew by half in a decade.

Before Parker came to Amherst, the admissions office feasted on Horatio Alger stories of the plucky undergraduate who defied the odds, but Parker measured success by statistics. He presented the faculty with a profile of the entering class that showed the number of tops-in-their-class students, minority students who benefited from race-conscious criteria, and students who received favored treatment as alumni offspring or athletes. There was also a sizable "miscellaneous" category for those admitted on a trustee's say-so or as a favor to a high school counselor who could be counted on to steer students Amherst's way.

This was the faculty's first behind-the-scenes look at how admissions actually worked, and they were appalled. They had assumed they were mostly teaching the best and the brightest—after all, Amherst turned away five out of six applicants—but only a third of the students were on the campus because of their intellect. Parker presented a second pie chart that showed the kind of class he favored. The percentage of students admitted on the basis of academics would increase by at least half—a figure that would include more students of color—and the number of athletes and legacies would shrink. While some old-line professors were allergic to this emphasis on diversity, most endorsed Parker's model. The pie chart also persuaded the trustees, who saw, for the first time, how admitting their favored candidates undercut the college's commitment to excellence.

THE SHIFT FROM RACE TO CLASS

By the turn of the millennium, Amherst College was leading the field in attracting minority students. Between 1985 and 2003—mach speed in the habitually conservative world of impossible-to-get-into schools—minority enrollment more than doubled, to nearly a third, an unheard-of accomplishment in highly selective college circles.

But more minority students didn't translate into more poor students. Many of them came from private schools, and while some had been plucked from underfunded public schools and given a couple of years of prep school education, more came from well-to-do families. Between 1967 and 2003, even as the percentage of minority students rose, the overall percentage of students from private schools remained essentially the same —39 percent in 1967, 38 percent in 2003—and more than half of the minority students' families could afford the full tab.

The number of students from low-income families ballooned after Tony Marx became president, in 2003. Beyond the campus, university presidents and influential journalists began to notice.[6]

"I wasn't qualified for the job," Marx tells me, and he issn't being modest. "I was a political scientist at Columbia. I had never been a provost or a dean. I hadn't even chaired a department. I was the longest of long shots." His worldview had been shaped by the years he spent in South Africa, where he helped found a college to educate blacks who had been denied the opportunity by apartheid. "If you can do this with kids who have suffered under apartheid, then you can't tell me we can't do better in the U.S., with all the resources we have," he told a *Bloomberg Business Week* reporter. The magazine titled the article "Campus Revolutionary."[7]

In 1999, Amherst became the nation's first college to eliminate loans for low-income students and replace them with scholarships, but the problem of class had not been addressed head-on. This was true nationwide. In *Equity and Excellence in American Higher Education*, economist William Bowen and his colleagues calculated that if students from poor families got the same break as students whose parents went to the same institution, the percentage of poor students at topflight schools would rise from 11 to 17 percent.[8] "The extent of wasted human capital is phenomenal," Georgetown economists Anthony Carnevale and Jeff Strohl concluded, after reviewing the evidence.[9]

Tony Marx calculated that, as president of one of the nation's top colleges, he could break the social class mold. "Schools like Amherst are reinforcing social inequality, and I'm not interested in being a custodian over a privileged place," he told the trustees at his job interview. "The college has a moral mandate and a democratic opportunity—and the financial firepower to make it happen."[10]

The trustees were primed to hear this message. "It was a consensus decision, and the equity motivation was the primary factor," recalls board chair Cullen Murphy. "Talent comes from everywhere, and should therefore be drawn from everywhere," Murphy wrote, in an article that ran in the alumni magazine. "This commitment, along with an abiding faith in the liberal arts, is one way to ensure that the college remains an acknowledged leader among its peers—that it maintains the position in relation to the larger society that it has long held. Equity, excellence, and effectiveness should be seen as one."[11]

Tony Marx was proposing a profound culture shift, a heavy lift at a school habituated to drafting elegant and often ignored committee reports rather than acting with urgency. He found himself sparring with a handful of professors who, as he puts it, "thought the president should fix the plumbing, raise money and do nothing else," and who didn't see social justice in their job description.

"The passive approach to letting talent rise is not working," Marx asserted at his first faculty meeting. "Just as blindness to race in itself could not alone redress the injustice of that discrimination, our blindness to need has not provided the opportunities for those most in need. The idea isn't to be a finishing school. It is to educate, and that shouldn't be easy. Education is about the distance traveled. If you take the smartest kids who come from the top schools and they end up the same, that's an expensive intervention for little output."

Most of the faculty agreed. "I don't have any patience for my colleagues—and I think there are very few now—who say we are sacrificing rigor," says chemistry professor David Hansen.

"Tom [Parker] and I threw the kitchen sink at it," Marx says. "We had to change financial aid policies, hire new staff, send them to different high schools, talk to more guidance counselors. We sent alumni into schools and students' homes and created an online mentoring program, run by current students, who gave prospective ones the lowdown on campus life." The college also started admitting transfers from community colleges, mostly from low-income families, who now account for 10 percent of the students.[12]

"The fact that we are not all the same is not merely a pleasant aspect of this college: it is an essential strength," the president explained to the entering freshman class in the fall of 2007. "We select and gather differences purposefully, and at some expense, precisely to build that strength. We build it because we learn more than if we were or behaved as if we were all the same. Your differences are also your best gifts to each other."

Deeds matched rhetoric—Amherst lost a third of its endowment during the Great Recession, but the drive to attract more poor students kept going. During Marx's years at the College, the number of Pell Grant recipients more than doubled, to 22 percent, the highest in the nation among top-ranked schools. The fear among conservative alumni that Amherst would suffer in the *U.S. News* rankings because of these changes turned out to be baseless. Amherst has consistently been ranked second among liberal arts colleges, behind only Williams, and it is first among its peers in the *Washington Monthly*'s social mobility rankings.[13]

A handful of top schools are following Amherst's lead. During Tony Marx's heyday, when Amherst was accelerating the number of Pell Grant students, Princeton was light years behind, but in recent years it has nearly caught up. Overall, however, the percentage of low-income students at world-class private universities has scarcely changed. And because states continue to cut funding for higher education, the percentage of Pell Grant undergraduates has actually declined at flagship public universities like Berkeley or Michigan, which enroll more undergraduates than the Ivy League universities and the Little Three colleges combined.[14]

FROM ACCESS TO INCLUSION

Tony Marx had an outsized vision—to turn Amherst College into a model of equity and excellence by attracting lots of highly talented, low-income students to the campus—and the fact that he pulled it off deserves kudos. But admitting these students has proven to be only the first step in realizing this vision. To make genuine inclusion a reality, new-gen undergraduates must believe that they belong there, that Amherst values their unique contributions to the culture.

The newcomers arrived at a campus whose manicured college green and weathered brick buildings emblematize its nineteenth-century WASP roots, a world of taken-for-granted wealth as strange and, for some of the newcomers, as uninviting as Jupiter. Marx took a laissez-faire approach— give these students a superb education and let them sort out the rest for themselves. "No one figured out even part of the plan before they had a population to define what the challenge would be," Dean of Students Alex

Vasquez tells me. There were too few advisers and counselors to whom these new students could turn, too few professors who understood that they had to reconfigure their courses.

"Students were dropped into the deep end of the pool without knowing how to swim," Tony Jack, one of this generation of students, observes. "Marx's attitude was: 'You will never have this opportunity again,'" adds chemistry professor Pat O'Hara. "But it wasn't that simple."

Biddy Martin, Tony Marx's successor, was called upon to address the question of how to bring the new-gen students into the heart of the College—how to turn a demographic fact into a demographic advantage.

"She didn't miss a beat," says Tom Parker. "What she brought is 'What's next?'"

Like Tony Marx, Biddy Martin was an improbable choice, though for different reasons. She was leaving the University of Wisconsin, one of the nation's leading public research institutions, a school twenty times bigger than Amherst. She would be the college's first female president, and that, as well as the fact that she is a lesbian, would have been deal-breakers a generation earlier, but those factors had become irrelevant. "She has formidable intellect and she's somebody who's very well respected," says Jide Zeitlin, chair of Amherst's board of trustees, explaining the decision. "This is somebody who's got an ability to range across the disciplines in a very formidable way. She also has two decades of deep leadership at highly respected institutions, so we're excited to benefit from that leadership experience."[15]

Biddy Martin knows all about the psychological tug of war between home and college that many students from poor families confront. She grew up in a small town in the foothills of Virginia's Blue Ridge Mountains, a place that was "racist, homophobic, anti-everything." Leaving home for college meant doing battle with her ultraconservative father, who was convinced that "the damn Yankees will ruin you."

"It was not easy to find my way, emotionally, between my family, who I was attached to, and what I was being exposed to at William and Mary," she tells me. She never felt fully accepted at a school where most of the students came from wealth, but that experience altered the course of her life. She earned her PhD at the University of Wisconsin, and became a German and Women's Studies professor at Cornell, where in 2000 she was selected to be the provost. Eight years later was named chancellor of the University of

Wisconsin. At both universities, making higher education more affordable and more welcoming to students from poor families was among her top priorities.

At Cornell, a university with a reputation for civility, Martin could focus on academic matters. But at Wisconsin she was sucked into the state's knife-fight politics, and it was those battle royals that did her in. She jumped at the chance to decamp to Amherst, where she could concentrate on what she held dear—strengthening the liberal arts and making student access, quality, and equality campus priorities.

OLD CULTURAL NORMS, NEW REALITIES

"Our task is to make Amherst a diverse intellectual community—with all three of these words equally relevant," Biddy Martin declares. To make this happen has meant probing every aspect of college life, from the classroom to the dorm room.

"The culture of the college is changing," says philosophy professor Jyl Gentzler. "People have been moved by the students' stories and want to do right by the stories. They used to think that if students failed they just weren't working hard. You cannot sell that story any more. We feel much more that when students aren't succeeding, it's our problem."

To tackle that problem, articles-of-faith ideas about teaching and learning had to be reassessed. *Rigor* is the go-to word among Amherst professors, but the form it has taken has sometimes gotten in the way of learning. Anachronistic rules—students cannot drop a course after the second week, students who don't take a full course load are treated as being on leave—only created anxiety. ("Needlessly hard-assed," is Dean of Faculty Catherine Epstein's tart verdict.) The widely shared belief that rigor could be measured in the length of reading assignments or the number of problem-sets keeps students in high-stress mode. Nationwide, the typical college student spends about seventeen hours a week studying, but many Amherst students study four times as much, and they name the library as their social center.[16] That's not a healthy sign, and it's one reason why a majority of them seek help from the campus counseling center.

The only way to teach that most professors are familiar with is how they were taught, through lectures. They believe lectures are "efficient," as chemistry professor David Hansen puts it. In fact, lectures do a bad job of imparting information and a worse job of turning students into problem-solvers—better to put the material online and let students absorb it at their own pace. Introductory courses were often designed with the expectation that the students would major in the discipline, and their content was off-putting to those who were looking through this disciplinary lens for the first time. A theory-drenched introductory economics course, for instance, did not speak to the novice who was curious about the relevance of the dismal science to real-world problems.

Many undergraduates from poor and minority backgrounds want to become doctors or programmers, but they stumble in the introductory math and chemistry courses. Students who went to renowned high schools and exclusive prep schools will have taken three years of math after calculus before coming to college, while others haven't gone beyond trigonometry. Some will have aced AP chemistry, while others have attended schools without a chemistry lab.

"I had taken biology my freshman year of high school. The only reason I didn't get a C was because I wrote a poem about penguins, so I got a B," said Eric Conklin, a transfer student from the University of Arizona, recruited by Amherst because of his prowess on the basketball court, tells me. "I show up to Amherst and on the first day, in intro to bio, the professor says: 'We're going to write down everything we know about mitochondria.' I go, mito-what? Students around me are writing paragraphs. They know this because they took AP bio their senior year in high school.

"My main goal was to go to med school, but students who come in from underserved schools squeak by with a C or a D, then they're thrown off the bus, told 'Your grades won't be good enough.' I got my first exams back in chem and bio and thought, dang, I'd never gotten a grade this low, what gives? I called my dad and said, 'I'm not doing so well here.' He said 'Keep going, it'll get better.' I was able to overcome the hurdle. I knew deep down that I could do it.

"I was able to rebound but lots of people aren't able to. I chose to stay in and study versus going out and drinking. There was a gap between myself and my classmates. I wanted to close that gap and eventually pass them. I consider myself to be so fortunate to be punched in the face and to recover due to my support system."

"There is in fact a gap," says chemistry professor Sheila Jaswal, who often talked with Conklin about the problem. "We didn't make the gap—it's out there. How do we provide the preparation the new generation of students needs to succeed?"

The one-size-fits-all model, with its outmoded assumption that students come equally well prepared, was gospel at Amherst. Cultural norms aren't easily uprooted, and professors had to be convinced that the payoff was worth the effort before changing their practice.

"Some of my colleagues think of calculus as the universal intelligence test," says math professor David Cox, "but it's not." Cox devised a class for students with weak math backgrounds that builds in the algebra they need to handle calculus. Similarly, David Hansen created a chemistry class that slows the pace of instruction, adds teaching assistants, and incorporates tutoring. And the economics department revamped its theory-drenched introductory course to entice novices into the field.

Like many colleges, Amherst has a quant center and a writing center, places where students can get unraveling an equation or drafting a paper. But unlike most colleges, there was faculty resistance to opening the centers, as well as opposition to using upperclassmen as tutors or TAs. "We should be doing all the teaching. Students can meet with us during office hours," they argued. They had students like Eric Conklin in mind. "I met with the professor the day after the exam. 'I failed,' I said. 'Help me not fail again.' He kept working with me the rest of the semester."

Amherst professors take office hours seriously—they may last eight hours a week, far longer than at most schools—and it hadn't dawned on them that some students might be intimidated. The dissenters eventually embraced the centers and the other academic buttresses when they realized their time would be freed up for bigger-picture conversations with their students.

When a survey found that a third of the students felt lonely and isolated, professors saw this as a counseling problem—the deficiencies had to be fixed, the students patched up. But faculty members have a responsibility as well, especially at a college where students take their studies so seriously, because the way they experience their education can shape their sense of themselves.

Things are changing. Hari Kumar, recruited by Biddy Martin to help professors redesign their courses, is showing them how to shift gears in the classroom, moving away from a deficit model, which emphasizes students' weaknesses, and toward a growth mindset model, which prizes tenacity. "We're not just learning about how to help underprepared students, but also about how we can get better at our job as teachers," says English professor Rhonda Cobham-Sander.

"I see teachers fall back in love with teaching," Kumar tells me. "They're reminded why they went into the profession in the first place."

Changing the faculty culture is one thing, influencing the ways students connect—or don't connect—with one another is an entirely different matter. The sharp divides of class and race are clear from the first hour at Amherst. One freshman emerges from a stretch limo, suitcase after suitcase carted into her dorm room by the driver, her mother busily decorating her room. Her roommate comes alone because her parents have to work. She gets off the Greyhound bus and walks to campus, carrying a battered suitcase. Down the corridor, a student lays down his prayer rug while his roommate installs a seventy-inch, flat-screen TV. The dorm rooms are small, and during the coming days, living in such close proximity, the roommates will learn a lot about one another's backgrounds.

These intersections do not occur serendipitously. This is part of our mission, Alex Vasquez tells parents of incoming freshmen. "Your children's lives are going to be uncomfortable—safe but uncomfortable. Otherwise we have failed."

"Who else can do that and get 8,000 applications?" he muses.

Orientation is meant to ease the transition to college life, and at Amherst part of this transition means living in a world more varied than most of the students have experienced, testing the limits of the heretical and forming relationships that no one in their old lives could comprehend. As eighteen-year-olds, many of them away from home for the first time, they are discarding old identities and trying on new ones. When Vasquez and his colleagues decide who will room together and who will go through orientation together, the fine hand of the social engineer is at work, putting a thumb on the scale of community-building.

Social learning is also baked into the freshman seminar that all the students must take. Whatever the theme—these range from "Experiments in Physics" to "Secrets and Lies" and "The Literature of Love"—the goal is the same: to give these students the tools of college-level critical thinking. And because the class is composed with an eye to diversity, with no more than one student from a foreign country and no more than one athlete from any sport, students get to know classmates they would otherwise never encounter.

Most of the sections add a session that gives students the opportunity to talk about their own lives. "What have you learned about yourself?" Austin Sarat, who started the program in 2014, asked them at the end of the term. "What was hard? How did you surprise yourself? What secrets do you want to share?" The intention, Sarat says, is "to show students they are not alone, and that we care about their personal lives." Talia Land says the class helped her realize she needed to reach for help. "If I keep avoiding conversations or keep avoiding asking for help or keep avoiding certain things [I will miss out]. . . . I don't want to get sentimental, but it's all going to go by before we know it," she said. "I'm going to miss this class a lot."[17]

The college keeps looking for ways to span the divides of race and class. The coaches have begun advising their players that they should leave their social cocoon and get to know other students. The placement office finds paid summer internships for students interested in careers in finance who lack the family connections that would gain them entrée. Coat-and-tie, red-and-white-wine, salad-and-dessert-fork dinners, to which all students are invited, prepare them for post-collegiate life. Even the configuration of the dining hall has been changed to disrupt cliquishness, with small round tables and booths replacing the long tables that football players had monopolized.

Like everything related to diversity at the college, much has been done and much remains undone in contributing to students' out-of-class experiences. "What matters most is that they believe they're getting a first-rate education, and that they feel that they belong," Biddy Martin tells me. "There's so much good intention among faculty and staff, but we need to get more systematic, using good information, with more hands on deck."

"I still struggle with feelings of inadequacy and social incompatibility specific to my experiences as a low-income, first-generation student," says Brittanie Lewis. "Your more fortunate peers will frustrate you with their well-meaning suggestion to just 'buy a new one' after you lose your coat; they may sadden you when they ask where your parents went to school, where your siblings want to go, why you seem so different from your entire family. Sometimes, you might feel you just don't belong on campus." She has some advice to students in the same situation: "I implore you to have confidence in the fact that you were chosen not only for your academic competency but also for the perspective you have to offer your peers and professors. You are now part of a conversation that would be lacking without your voice. Speak even louder, and help others understand a life story they may not have considered before they met you."[18]

"The stories are here, the people are here, the resources are here," says Norm Jones, whom Biddy Martin hired in 2016 as the college's first diversity officer. "We need to do a better job of connecting the dots."

A 2017 Curriculum Committee report noted that while 95 percent of Amherst students graduate, the figure is 7 to 10 percent lower for new-gen students. "Some students, especially male students of color, aren't thriving," Jones notes. "They aren't leaving, but some are just surviving. They tell the counselors they feel trapped. We need space and airtime to get a read on how those students are doing. My rigor may be your suicidal ideation. If your contribution is your brown skin it won't dawn on me to talk about your STEM research. The students say, 'I would give a lot for you to inquire about what's in my brain.'"

GETTING IT RIGHT

Ask the alumni of any school what they remember most about their college years, and usually the first thing that comes to mind is not their courses or the great professor they had. It's their friendships. There are limits to how much a college, even one as social-engineering-minded as Amherst, can do to coax eighteen- to twenty-two-year-olds into making frienships that cross the lines of race and class.

The students I spoke with were passionate about the entanglements of race and ethnicity, class and gender. Students of color discussed how they had to justify their actions, to prove that they belonged, as if they were Ralph Ellison's *Invisible Man*, noticed but not seen. They were tired of having to educate white students, of having lab partners who didn't respect them. Their classmates were clueless about the two- and three-job lives that many of them led, earning money so that their families could pay the cable TV bill. Women spoke of men who interrupted them in class, ignored them in labs, and fondled them at parties. A few of them, like George Young—English major, decent pitcher, chair of the Black Students Union, "good at code-switching"—acted as a bridge among these factions, but there was only so much those students could accomplish.

Athletics plays an important role in spawning these social tensions, Dean Rick Lopez tells me. At elite universities like Duke, it's taken for granted that athletes live cosseted lives, housed in separate dorms and intensely prepped for their courses. But at Amherst, where nearly a third of the students are varsity athletes, many students want the entire college to be a strong community. The unhappiness that stems from feeling left out of a charmed circle—of not belonging—is palpable.

For an eighteen-year-old who comes to college knowing no one, worried about making friends, the team is the logical place to turn. Athletes—especially the football, baseball, and field hockey players, mostly the sons and daughters of professionals and mostly white—form cliques that contrive to live in the same dorms and party together. They organize the off-campus fraternities and sororities that the college strives to eliminate. They share tips on what courses to take and what internships to pursue. They congregate at separate tables in the dining commons. They dominate the large dormitory suites, and monopolize the biggest party space. "When the dorm with the biggest suites was torn down, I got a letter from a parent of a football player," Biddy Martin tells me. "'How dare you get rid of *our* space for parties. We demand that you replace it.'"

The majority of athletes come from privileged backgrounds," says Eric Conklin, the University of Arizona transfer who starred on Amherst's basketball team. "Is there a divide? Absolutely. If you're athletic, you're deemed more socially competent. If I was not on a sports team, I wouldn't have anywhere to go on a Saturday night."

This isn't a two-separate-worlds tale—the quarterback might be a thespian, the point guard might be pre-med—but the problematic place that athletics occupies has prompted the drafting of two reports by trustees, faculty, and students in the past fifteen years. Athletics has been an irritant for some professors, who lodge complaints about "the athletes" in faculty meetings. The fact that most of them are white adds another layer of separation, another source of tension. That frustration prompted women of color to found an organization called NARP—nonathletic real people.

"You say you recruit the best and brightest from all over the world," says Alex Vasquez, relaying what a student told him. "You tell us all that we're unique snowflakes—that's why I'm going to contribute so much. But every unique football snowflake gets to have snowflakes just like them and I don't get to have any snowflakes who are just like me."

There's no doubting the genuineness of the students' laments or the depth of their feeling. But, as Vasquez points out, "this generation expects the adults to fix their problems. I ask them, 'Do you want a forty-five-year-old dean to tell you what your social life should be?'" Thrown together for four years, Amherst students live in an echo-chamber of discontent, where, as Alida Mitlau observes, praise is suspect and disaffection is raised to an art form.

"It's my favorite thing about Amherst—to be living in this experiment," she adds. "I'm middle class, from Minneapolis. I try to experience all the different social groups, and what they're like, try to talk to as many different people as possible. It's interesting to see the different baselines of understanding. Some people don't want to deal with it, just talk to those people who are like them. I spent an hour talking to a white, middle-class football player. He was saying he thinks he's part of the most oppressed group on campus. How do you tell him 'You don't know anything'?"

"Amherst has not changed," a disillusioned George Young contends. "The Uprising made no difference." He's wrong, though, for the College keeps moving in the direction of equity. In 2017, it approved a Latinx and Latin-American Studies major, which was one of the protestors' demands. The freshmen seminars, with their talk-to-me sessions; the not-so-random dorm assignments; the wiser counseling; the STEM courses that have been revamped so that less-prepared students can catch up; the nudges from the coaches; the new dorm, designed to break down social boundaries—it all adds up. And while it is easy to make fun of gawky gestures at inclusion like the redesign of the dining hall, those decisions probably matter as well.

"Amherst is doing work that isn't even being imagined anyplace else," American Studies professor Leah Schmalzbauer tells me. Having taught for a decade at Montana State before coming to the college, she brings an outsider's perspective. "If we can't have these conversations here, where else will they happen?"

It's easy enough to make people feel at home when they're more or less alike, as used to be the case at Amherst. But the college has remade itself as the Flying Wallendas of academe. Having opened the doors wide to new-gen undergraduates, it is setting in motion tightrope-walking moments that its students may never again experience and asking its professors to learn how to educate students who bring radically different life histories to their classrooms.

No wonder that success always looms out of reach, and that each time a milestone is reached another challenge emerges. At a school like Amherst College, committed to making diversity work, the task of creating a place to which everyone feels that they belong never ends.

8

ENDING THE DROPOUT SCANDAL
Where Are the Leaders?

Ask those in the know to identify the nation's top campus leaders, and the same names come up time and again—Nancy Cantor at Rutgers-Newark, Freeman Hrabowski at the University of Maryland-Baltimore County, and Michael Crow at Arizona State. Each of them has formulated a compelling vision of the Good University, and each has been relentless in transforming that vision into reality.

"The fox knows many things but the hedgehog knows one big thing"— philosopher Isaiah Berlin's much-quoted aphorism sums up the chief difference between Nancy Cantor and Freeman Hrabowski, classic hedgehogs, and Michael Crow, the quintessential fox.

Nancy Cantor's *idée fixe* is to give a top-drawer education to the type of student that prestige-minded schools shy away from—inner-city undergraduates with less-than-impeccable high school records, but with the potential to become leaders. Freeman Hrabowski has concentrated on raising the number of minority STEM graduates, and during his quarter-century as president the university has trained a cadre of distinguished black and Latino scientists, doctors, and engineers.

Michael Crow is designing what he envisions as a model for twenty-first-century higher education. The university, biggest in the nation, has expanded on steroids, "finding and educating a fantastically talented cross-section of the society," moving from what Crow describes as a faculty-centric culture to a student-centric culture, increasing the number of graduates and shrinking the equity gap. Meanwhile, Arizona State has enrolled more National Merit scholars than Stanford or MIT, graduated more Fulbright Scholars than Harvard, and launched multi-million-dollar multidisciplinary research initiatives in fields that range from bioenergetics to humane cities.[1]

These super-chiefs give Ted Talks, write opinion pieces for the *New York Times,* and get invited to the White House. In 2012, *Time Magazine* named Freeman Hrabowski one of the world's 100 most influential people. They are larger-than-life figures, the Steve Jobses of higher education. But as the accounts of punching-above-their-weight colleges and universities show, it doesn't take a Mensa member to captain a high-performing university.

Many of the presidents and provosts at the schools we visited took on that position almost by happenstance. Mark Becker, at Georgia State, had never even attended a faculty senate meeting when a colleague convinced him that he could have an outsized impact as an administrator. David Laude had been a chemistry teacher par excellence at the University of Texas when he was tapped to be a dean and then the graduation rate champion. John Hitt, at the Central Florida University, was deep into his research when the university came calling. "People were asking me about administrative jobs, assistant and associate dean of this or that, and I resisted for a while."

What's wanted, nationwide, are many more college presidents and provosts like these, dedicated to putting students' concerns, not institutional prestige, atop their to-do list, as well as the dollars needed to underwrite this work. Without basic change in how universities are run, there's no end in sight to the dropout scandal.

At each of the institutions we have looked at, forceful leadership is driving the campaign to improve graduation rates and close the equity gap. Each of these top administrators has:

*an abiding commitment to make student access and success their institution's top priority[2]

*a focus on getting their students engaged in their studies and connected
to the campus

*a willingness to question "this is how it's always been done" cultural
orthodoxies

*the recognition that decisions should be based on data rather than hunch

*the skill to create a compelling vision for change and evoke a sense of
urgency for that change

*the tenacity to turn that vision into on-the-ground reality.

When institutions get serious about the dropout crisis, the consequences
can be dramatic. The big state universities in the eleven-member University
Innovation Alliance that followed the lead of Georgia State, and Arizona State
(the University of Central Florida and Cal State Long Beach among them)
graduated 25 percent more low-income students over the span of three years.[3]

Because the dropout problem is really a bundle of concerns, the leaders
of the schools we've looked at rely on an array of managerial styles and tools.
Mark Becker and Tim Renick at Georgia State, John Hitt at the University
of Central Florida, Biddy Martin and Tony Marx at Amherst, Nancy Cantor
at Rutgers-Newark, and David Dowell at Long Beach State concentrated
authority at the center. Brian Jersky and Jane Conley at Long Beach State,
and Bill Powers and David Laude at the University of Texas, adopted a
"trust-but-verify" approach that left greater discretion in the hands of the
deans. Sandy Shugart at Valencia has spun off a host of "Big Ideas," enlisting
colleagues who share his enthusiasms to fill in the details. Similarly, John
Mogulescu, who heads higher education's version of a skunkworks at CUNY,
has generated a constant flow of innovations. But because of his unique position in the administrative hierarchy and the resistance of some campus presidents, he has had to rely on the backing of a succession of chancellors to put
those innovations into effect.

Most of these senior administrators initially concentrated on constructing
an exoskeleton of student support, rather than addressing what transpires
inside the classroom, using data analytics, proactive advising, mini-grants,
learning communities, block scheduling, and the like to achieve their goals.[4]
The likelihood of faculty opposition, couched as an intrusion on their academic freedom, makes such prudence a virtue in the initial stages of reform.
But there are clearcut limits to what this hands-off approach to teaching can
accomplish.

Confronted with the imperative of expansion and the reality of a tight-squeeze budget, John Hitt relied on an array of carrots and sticks to nudge the faculty into designing thousands of carefully crafted online classes, enabling the institution to grow without sacrificing quality. Bill Powers rejected the advice of his cautious colleagues and reengineered the curriculum to emphasize writing and critical thinking, obliging students to think outside the confines of their major. As graduation rates stalled at Georgia State, Tim Renick and Mark Becker recognized that the high percentage of Ds and Fs in the biggest first-year courses represented a formidable barrier to graduation, and replacing the time-honored lecture with a more hands-on approach looked to be the most promising way of removing it.

Although scores of best-sellers like *The Seven Habits of Highly Effective People* and thousands of articles with come-on titles like "100 Qualities of a Leader" have been written on the topic, no single model of the ideal leader has emerged. Distinctive styles work for different personalities—no-nonsense Mark Becker reshaped a low-ambition institution and so did the less hard-charging John Hitt. Shifting circumstances can also determine how top administrators behave. With a chancellor as audacious as CUNY's Matthew Goldstein to back him, John Mogulescu had considerable latitude to try out new ideas. A fiscal crisis gave Mark Becker the opportunity to effect large-scale changes in the university's priorities.

THE ROLE OF FOUNDATIONS IN POWERING REFORM

These senior administrators, while admired by their colleagues for their boldness, remain rarities in the timid, status-quo-oriented world of higher education. Can the president's job description be rewritten to stress students' performance? Is it possible to shift the dynamic, away from exclusivity and toward inclusion . . . away from dependence on *US News* rankings, which reinforce existing wealth, and toward rating systems, like those of the *New York Times* and *Washington Monthly*, that place a premium on equity . . . away from college presidents' "trust-us" claims and toward greater accountability for results?[5] Can meaningful reform be carried out at a statewide or even national scale?

Foundations are bankrolling an array of promising strategies.

The Lumina Foundation is helping states devise funding formulas that are based not on the number of students who start college but on the number who graduate and the quality of their education. "Influencing the influencers" is how Foundation president Jamie Meresotis summarizes its game plan.

The Gates Foundation aims at slicing through the present-day fog of data by creating a reporting system that can deliver apples-to-apples comparisons regarding how well universities perform on access, cost, and outcomes. With that information in hand, better measures of accountability can be devised.

Complete College America focuses on the money-saving strategy of expanding the number of students who earn a bachelor's degree in four, rather than six, years. Its agenda of campus initiatives, tried-and-true approaches like pressing students to enroll full-time, has been endorsed by a host of universities as well as state higher education systems.

The Education Trust generates statistics that can influence institutional decisions. Its College Report Card shows how well a university stacks up against similar schools in the percentage of students it graduates and its effectiveness in eliminating the equity gap. "The Report Card holds up a mirror to colleges—'Maybe there's something we can do better,'" John King, who runs the organization, tells me. "By moving data on equity to the mainstream, we are influencing the policy conversation."

TRAINING A NEW GENERATION OF LEADERS

Tim Renick was thinking aloud about the uphill battle to remake the norms and customs of a university. "Faculty and administrators are entrenched by academic privilege. Their experience in the classroom makes them feel confident about themselves. It's a big battle to shift their belief that, when low-income students graduate at lower rates, the fault lies with the public schools, not themselves. Try doing something different and some professors and administrators will have a rationale for not doing it. To accomplish anything, you need a powerful conviction and a thick skin."

Leading researchers agree with Renick's diagnosis. When Michael Cohen, at the University of Michigan, and James March, at Stanford, laid out the widely cited "systemic-anarchic" perspective of organizational decision-making—dubbed the Garbage Can Model—the university was their prime example.[6]

This is where the Aspen Institute enters the picture. It has made a multimillion dollar bet that, with passion as the indispensable starting point for a prospective change-agent president, the skills required to overcome institutional inertia and become a powerhouse leader can be taught. The Institute has concentrated on community colleges because that's where most new-gen undergraduates enroll and where the dropout crisis is worst. If the equity gap is going to be closed, these schools must play a big part.

"We need a national strategy to get leaders who know how to improve their students' lives," says Josh Wyner, who runs the Aspen initiative. "They need to build a culture that's student-success oriented, to determine the most strategic use of their resources and to build partnerships with the public schools, universities and employers in their community."

In the autumn of 2017, forty community college administrators came to Airlie House, a turn-of-the-century manse situated on three hundred acres in the verdant Virginia countryside, for a week-long conference on leadership, the second of three such meetings. The Fellows, as Aspen calls them, are newly minted college presidents or else on a glide path to a presidency. Although their background and experiences vary—some of them grew up in suburbia and went to private academies, others were raised in the barrio and were educated in dropout-factory high schools—all of them are driven by the desire to give their students a better life.

"How do we help our students be successful when they are struggling to acquire basic needs, like food and shelter?" That's what haunts John Mosby, a senior administrator at Mission College, in Silicon Valley, where billionaires live only a few miles from homeless encampments. "How can they move forward when they are just trying to survive? There are a lot of students who are suffering. It's just overwhelming. It keeps me up at night."

Cynthia Oliva, who runs the student affairs office at Pasadena City College, outside Los Angeles, reflects on her own sleepless nights. "We have the potential to help thousands more students reach their goals. I have this sense of urgency, and I get frustrated by how long it takes to make deep structural changes that can really move the needle. I'm a Latina and I know what's at stake and why we have to push forward. Students are out there struggling. I feel an obligation to our community to change their circumstances."

Charlene Nunley, the former president of Montgomery College, outside Washington, DC, and a mentor in the Aspen program, describes an event at which she found herself seated next to a state legislator. "He looked at me and said: 'You're doing such a great job; you're going to be president of a great university.' Without even thinking I replied: 'Why would I want to do that? I get to change people's lives every day. If they go to the university they're going to do fine anyway.' He was so impressed that he checked out what we were doing and drafted a bill to increase funding for the community colleges."

To enliven the proceedings, Wyner recruited a handful of rock-star lecturers like psychologist Claude Steele, whose research on "stereotype threat" led to the design of brief experiences to instill a sense of belonging and a growth mindset. "I was like, seriously, at a Justin Bieber concert," John Mosby gushes. For the most part, though, these are roll-up-your sleeves sessions led by seasoned practitioners. Discussions of leadership in higher education are plagued by theorizing of dubious worth and the rosy reminisces of former presidents, but at Airlie House the agenda is short on theory, long on practical information and case studies.

"We're deep into discussions with presidents and chancellors who are talking about real-life issues, giving us the story and challenging us to solve these problems from the president's perspective," Mosby explains.

Bob Templin, the former president of Northern Virginia Community College System, posed a problem he faced when he headed a campus. "You have a student who has been admitted into a mental hospital. A police officer who knows you comes to you with the student's diary, which has a detailed description of a mass murder taking place on your campus. You go to your legal team and they advise you that there is no legal way that you can bar the student from campus because the diary was obtained illegally, the police officer should not have taken it from the student and should not have given to you because of federal regulations that require the confidential handling of protected health information. They advise you that if you do ban the student, you expose yourself to a potential lawsuit. It is Friday and the student is going to be released over the weekend and has class scheduled on Monday. What do you do?"

Kenneth Ender, the president of Harper College, located outside Chicago, offered the Fellows a very different challenge. "Twenty-five CEOs from local companies were beating down my door, begging for help. They've got three hundred manufacturing jobs they could fill now, but they don't have the trained workers, and because lots of workers are near retirement age the situation is going to get worse. The college doesn't have the manufacturing equipment, and you'd need to invest upwards of $3 million to support this program. What do you do?"

During the ensuing conversation, the Fellows pondered how to get the manufacturers to pay for some of the equipment needed for the training course. They discussed establishing apprenticeship models to guarantee jobs as well as making sure program was up to date. (In reality, Enders told the group, the training program was launched with financial backing from the manufacturers.)

The Fellows wanted a chance to get feedback from their colleagues on how they had handled challenges of their own. In a presentation titled "Majority Minority Students, Educational Equity and Parity in Outcomes," Cynthia Olivo presented an equity tool she developed, noting the difficulties she had in familiarizing faculty with the tool and getting her colleagues on board.

Josh Wyner doesn't sugarcoat the predicaments of a college president. Quite the contrary. "Leaders are programmed to tout what's great, but a president needs to use data in order to build urgency around specific problems, like the black-white graduation gap, and say, 'That's not okay.' You're not blaming anyone, but you have to create a sense of despair before you push for change. Then you can rally the campus—that is the work of leadership. The faculty must be part of the solution," says Charlene Nunley. "It's absolutely crucial for leaders to take on questions involving teaching and learning. You need to show faculty the evidence about the retention of students and get them to take an honest look at what's happening before you can make progress."

Valencia College president Sandy Sanger, a role model for these fledgling administrators, was one of the speakers. "Change is a cocktail," he told them. "One part despair and three parts hope."

Aspen is giving these youthful administrators a management toolkit that's purpose-built to foster and take advantage of this sense of urgency. "You need to be an internal change agent," explains Wyner. "You need to know how to move an institution that is very decentralized, how to organize people around big ideas and how to convince the faculty to concentrate not on particular programs or enrollment figures but return on investment—the cost of each degree, not each student."[7]

In promoting their agenda, the Fellows are urged to seek out allies among the professors with the know-how to make big-ticket introductory courses more user-friendly. They are also taught how to collaborate with community partners like the public schools, which can prepare their students for college-level math and English; nearby universities, which can simplify the transfer process; and local companies, which can offer their graduates decent jobs.

"We'll get to a tipping point in the next five or six years, when we get a hundred presidents in the field," Wyner predicts. "That's a real anchor for reform across the entire landscape."

THE END GAME

In a 2017 report on black student success, the Education Trust singled out Wayne State as a "Hall of Shame" institution. Its overall graduation rate, 33 percent, was barely half that of similar schools. Even worse, just one black student in ten earned a degree. "Why didn't that set everyone's hair on fire?" wonders Bill Moses, head of the Kresge Foundation's education program, who watched the disaster unfold. He answered his own question: "Because no one was held accountable."

When I talk about the dropout scandal, this is the kind of institution I have in mind. But things at Wayne State turned around when the university recruited a president and a provost zealous about getting bachelor's degrees in their students' hands and knowledgeable about converting their dedication into durable change. The duo borrowed from Georgia State's playbook, to great effect—between 2014 and 2017, the graduation rate rose from 33 to 47 percent, perhaps the most striking improvement nationwide. A fifth of the black undergraduates earned a bachelor's degree that year—still unacceptably low, but double the figure for 2014.

"Making changes means being relentless," President Roy Wilson emphasizes.[8]

Georgia State and the other schools we've highlighted in our campus journey are national models. Wayne State and the Innovation Alliance partners have proven apt pupils. But when are the other universities that the Education Trust report identified for failure—Auburn University, Long Island University, and the University of Wisconsin-Milwaukee—going to face up to the miseducation of their students?

"The force of inertia is strong, and other presidents cannot believe this is possible to fix," Bill Moses tells me. "This goes to the core of who they are and how they see their jobs."

"How can we take $40,000 from a student, knowing that he's likely to fail?" he added. "Are we like for-profit colleges that don't care about the outcomes, only the revenue?"

ACKNOWLEDGMENTS

I envy authors who, when they launch into a writing project, have firmly in mind a sequence of books on the same topic. That's not been my modus operandi. Instead, a big policy puzzle presents itself, seemingly by chance, and I take the bait. So, too, here.

In a conversation some years ago, my old friend Hank Levin suggested that I look into an initiative that had slashed the college dropout rate. When Hank suggests, I listen, and the program—the ASAP model at CUNY—led me into the world of student success. I dug into the field, and after learning about Georgia State's remarkable accomplishments—improving graduation rates and making mincemeat of the opportunity gap—I was hooked.

What these two institutions had accomplished offered proof that it was possible to dramatically boost graduation rates. Why weren't other institutions doing the same? Why were the futures of tens of millions of lives truncated when solutions were at hand? To me, this is not just a policy problem but a moral issue as well.

Like my public policy colleagues, I'm interested in what works. That's what led me on a year-long journey to some of the most impressive colleges and universities in the nation, schools that have made student success a priority. It's a journey that I could never have undertaken without the generous support of the Spencer Foundation and the Lumina Foundation.

The Goldman School of Public Policy at Berkeley has been my intellectual home for more than four decades, and I've been fortunate in having whip-smart graduate students to work with. The RAs with whom I worked over the course of two years—Vellori Adithi, A. J. Herrmann, and Hannah Melnicoe—did more than an author can reasonably expect. They pulled together mountains of background material. They helped me determine which colleges and universities to focus on. One of them joined me on each field trip, and our conversations during those visits informed my thinking. They reviewed the draft chapters, and their comments sharpened my perspective.

Parker Goyer, a Stanford postdoctoral student and top-drawer researcher in her own right, superbly summarized the voluminous research on resiliency-promoting strategies. Rachel Roberson, a graduate student at the School of Education at Berkeley, arranged interviews and accompanied me on the field trip to the University of Texas.

I was tutored by some of the smartest people in higher education, including Tom Bailey, Henry Brady, Tony Bryk, Ben Castleman, Geoffrey Cohen, Carol Dweck, Kati Haycock, Anthony Jack, Henry Levin, Jamie Meresotis, Pedro Noguera, Marcelo Suarez-Orozco, Vincent Tinto, Greg Walton, Josh Wyne, and Mark Yudof. Paul Tough's *New York Times* article, "Who Gets to Graduate?", contributed to my interest in the topic. Invariably, authors omit individuals who contributed their insights; my apologies to all of you.

To borrow a famous line, I've always depended on the kindness of strangers. So too here—I would have been lost without the help I received from pivotal figures on each campus I visited. They provided briefing material, organized the visits, arranged many of the interviews and patiently answered scores of questions. My special thanks to Donna Linderman and John Mogulescu at CUNY, Tim Renick at Georgia State, Rick Schell at the University of Central Florida, Sandy Shugart and Joyce Romano at Valencia College, David Laude at the University of Texas, Brian Jersky at Cal State-Long Beach, Nancy Cantor and Timothy Eatman at Rutgers University, Biddy Martin and Catherine Epstein at Amherst College, and Monica Brockmeyer at Wayne State University. Conversations with Arizona State University president Michael Crow, Princeton University president Christopher Eisgruber, and Franklin and Marshall president Dan Porterfield added depth to my understanding of the higher education landscape.

Good editors are a godsend. Bruce Headlam, Honor Jones, and Sewell Chan at the *New York Times*, and Susan Brenneman at the *Los Angeles Times* sharpened my thinking and honed my prose.

My agent, James Levine, has been a passionate supporter of the project, whose comments have made for a better book.

Oxford University Press has been the perfect editorial home. The conventional wisdom is that editors are in the acquisitions business; after that, the author is on his own. My experience at Oxford couldn't have been more different. James Cook nurtured the book proposal through the Scylla and Charybdis of the editorial review process. He gave a fine-grained reading to a succession of drafts, and his suggestions led me to rethink and refine my prose (how he managed this feat while tending to triplets is a mystery). Meenakshi Venkat did a scrupulous job of copyediting. Cheryl Merritt shepherded the manuscript through the production process.

As ever, Rhea Wilson, my close friend and editor par excellence, delivered richly-detailed critiques of each of the chapters. What mattered even more was her uncanny ability to make me recognize what I implicitly knew but hadn't figured out how to express.

Niko Laine brought an outsider's keen perspective to the chapters, taking on the invaluable role of the educated lay reader. He has also changed the arc of my life, incalculably for the better.

NOTES

INTRODUCTION

1. See Chapter 5 for a discussion of the University of Texas's efforts to boost the four-year graduation rate.
2. Meghan Kehoe, "The College Dropout," *Femsplain*, Apr. 2015, https://femsplain.com/the-college-dropout-8448f907a1e8.
3. Geoffrey Widdison, "What Are Some Non-Success Stories of College Dropouts?," *Quora*, January 15, 2015, https://www.quora.com/What-are-some-non-success-stories-of-college-dropouts.
4. Kavitha Cardoza, "First-Generation College Students Are Not Succeeding in College, and Money Isn't the Problem," *Washington Post*, January 20, 2016, https://www.washingtonpost.com/posteverything/wp/2016/01/20/first-generation-college-students-are-not-succeeding-in-college-and-money-isnt-the-problem/?utm_term=.2b3990467f51.
5. "Education and Lifetime Earnings," *Social Security Office of Retirement Policy*, November 2015, https://www.ssa.gov/retirementpolicy/research/education-earnings.html.
6. Judith Scott-Clayton, *The Looming Student Loan Default Crisis Is Worse Than We Thought* (Washington, DC: Brookings, 2018), https://www.brookings.edu/research/the-looming-student-loan-default-crisis-is-worse-than-we-thought/; Robert Zimmer, "The Myth of the Successful College Dropout: Why It Could Make Millions of Young Americans Poorer," *The Atlantic*, March 1, 2013, https://www.theatlantic.com/business/archive/2013/03/the-myth-of-the-successful-college-dropout-why-it-could-make-millions-of-young-americans-poorer/273628/.
7. Mark Schneider and Lu (Michelle) Yin, *The High Cost of Low Graduation Rates: How Much Does Dropping Out of College Really Cost?* (Washington, DC: American Institutes of Research, August 2011), https://www.air.org/sites/default/files/downloads/report/AIR_High_Cost_of_Low_Graduation_Aug2011_0.pdf.
8. David Leonhardt, "A Winning Political Issue Hiding in Plain Sight," *New York Times*, March 18, 2018, https://www.nytimes.com/2018/03/18/opinion/education-campaign-issue.html; "The Myth of the Successful College Dropout."

The crowd-pleasing idea of making college free is no answer, because the challenge isn't getting students to enroll, but making sure they earn a degree. "Free college is politically popular," Harvard economist David Deming points out, "yet lower prices do not directly address the main crisis in U.S. higher education—low completion rates. Increasing college completion rates will require more than just cutting prices—we must also improve the quality of the education students receive." David Deming, *Increasing College Completion with A Federal Higher Education Matching Grant* (Washington, DC: Brookings, 2017), https://www.brookings.edu/research/increasing-college-completion-with-a-federal-higher-education-matching-grant/.

9. "Signature 14 Completing College: A National View of Student Completion Rates—Fall 2011 Cohort," NSC Research Center, December 13, 2017, https://nscresearchcenter.org/signaturereport14/. These data, from the National Student Clearinghouse, include all degree-seeking students who start college in the fall semester and graduate within six years. Unlike the more frequently cited Postsecondary Education Data System (IPEDS), these data include students who transfer as well as those who graduate from the institution at which they initially enrolled. See Clifford Adelman, "Do We Really Have a Dropout Problem?," *Change: The Magazine of Higher Learning*, 2008; George Kuh et al., "Unmasking the Effects of Student Engagement on First-Year College Grades and Persistence," *Journal of Higher Education*, vol. 79, no. 52, 540–563 (2008).

10. "Completing College: A National View of Student Attainment Rates—Fall 2009 Cohort," NSC Research Center, Nov. 16, 2015, https://nscresearchcenter.org/signaturereport10/.

11. "Graduation Rate," *OECD Data*, 2018, https://data.oecd.org/eduatt/graduation-rate.htm; Mark Schneider, *The Costs of Failure Factories in American Higher Education* (Washington, DC: American Enterprise Institute, 2009), http://www.aei.org/publication/the-costs-of-failure-factories-in-american-higher-education/.

12. "Fast Facts," National Center for Education Statistics, https://nces.ed.gov/fastfacts/display.asp?id=40.

13. Tamara Hiler and Lanae Erickson Hatalsky, *What Free Won't Fix: Too Many Public Colleges Are Dropout Factories* (Washington, DC: Third Way, August 11, 2016), https://www.thirdway.org/report/what-free-wont-fix-too-many-public-colleges-are-dropout-factories.

14. In a 2017 survey, about half of students said they paid some of the bill. About one-third used their current income and one-quarter used their savings. Katie Lobosco, "How the Average Family Pays for College," *CNN Money*, July 18, 2017, https://money.cnn.com/2017/07/17/pf/college/how-to-pay-for-college/index.html.

15. Richard Arum and Josipa Roksa, *Academically Adrift: Limited Learning on College Campuses* (Chicago: University of Chicago Press, 2011).

16. Only 20 percent of faculty cite institutional factors, as distinguished from students' characteristics, as a root cause of failure. Abour H. Cherif et al., *Why Do Students Fail? Faculty's Perspective* (Chicago: Higher Learning Commission, 2014).

17. Nicholas Hillman, *Why Performance-Based College Funding Doesn't Work* (Washington, DC: Century Foundation, 2016), https://tcf.org/content/report/why-performance-based-college-funding-doesnt-work/?agreed=1.

18. Byron White, "The Myth of the College-Ready Student," *Inside Higher Education*, March 21, 2016, https://www.insidehighered.com/views/2016/03/21/instead-focusing-college-ready-students-institutions-should-become-more-student.

19. Ben Miller and Phuong Lee, "College Dropout Factories," *Washington Monthly*, July 2010.
20. Raj Chetty et al., "Mobility Report Cards: The Role of Colleges in Intergenerational Mobility," NBER Working Paper No. 23618 (July 2017).
21. As Chapter 7, which focuses on Amherst College, points out, merely having abundant resources is no guarantee of student success.
22. "Graduation Rate from First Institution Attended for First-Time, Full-Time Bachelor's Degree-Seeking Students at 4-Year Postsecondary Institutions, By Race/Ethnicity, Time to Completion, Sex, Control of Institution, and Acceptance Rate: Selected Cohort Entry Years, 1996 Through 2009," *Digest of Education Statistics*, October 2016, https://nces.ed.gov/programs/digest/d16/tables/dt16_326.10.asp; "What Free Won't Fix: Too Many Public Colleges Are Dropout Factories."
23. Andrew Nichols and Denzel Evans-Bell, *A Look at Black Student Success: Identifying Top- and Bottom-Performing Institutions* (Washington, DC: Education Trust, March 1, 2017), https://edtrust.org/resource/black-student-success/.

    Stanford economist Raj Chetty and his colleagues at the Economic Opportunity Project have identified a number of universities, among them the City College of New York and Cal State-Los Angeles, that are making good on the promise of economic mobility, moving youth from poor families into the middle class. "Mobility Report Cards: The Role of Colleges in Intergenerational Mobility." Raj Chetty et al., "Mobility Report Cards: The Role of Colleges in Intergenerational Mobility," NBER Working Paper No. 23618 (July 2017).
24. "CIRP Freshman Survey," Higher Education Research Institute, 2018, https://heri.ucla.edu/cirp-freshman-survey/.
25. Robert T. Reason, Patrick Terrenzini, and Robert Domingo, "Developing Social and Personal Competence in the First Year of College," *Review of Higher Education*, vol. 30, no. 3, 271–299 (Spring 2007), https://muse.jhu.edu/article/211489.
26. Randi S. Levitz, Lee Noel, and Beth J. Richter, "Strategic Moves for Retention Success," *New Directions for Higher Education* (Vol. 1999, Issue 108, pgs. 31–49). Chapter 8 focuses on the importance of leadership in boosting student success.
27. Editorial Board, "Give Money to College Students Who Need It: Merit-based Scholarships Hurt the Poor," *Bloomberg View*, February 28, 2018, https://www.bloomberg.com/view/articles/2018-02-28/merit-scholarships-don-t-help-college-students-who-need-it-most; Steven Burd, "The Troubling Use of 'Merit Aid' at Public Flagships and Research Universities," *Hechinger Report*, April 27, 2016, https://hechingerreport.org/troubling-use-merit-aid-public-flagships-research-universities/.
28. Vincent Tinto, *Completing College: Rethinking Institutional Action* (Chicago: University of Chicago Press, 2012), pages 116–117.
29. "Strategic Moves for Retention Success"; Chapter 8 focuses on the importance of leadership in boosting student success.
30. Brad Phillips, "College Completion Goals Need Bigger Thinking, Bolder Action," *Huffington Post*, December 16, 2015, https://www.huffingtonpost.com/brad-c-phillips/college-completion-goals-_b_8816938.html.

31. Gregor Aisch et al., "Some Colleges Have More Students from the Top 1 Percent Than the Bottom 60," *New York Times*, January 18, 2017, https://www.nytimes.com/interactive/2017/01/18/upshot/some-colleges-have-more-students-from-the-top-1-percent-than-the-bottom-60.html.

32. Seventy-seven percent of students who were enrolled in degree-granting institutions in the fall of 2015 were enrolled at public institutions. Students in two-year degree programs are more likely to be enrolled in public institutions than their counterparts who are working towards four-year degrees: 96 percent of students in two-year degree programs were enrolled in public institutions vs. 66 percent of those in four-year degree programs. "Total Undergraduate Fall Enrollment in Degree-Granting Postsecondary Institutions, by Attendance Status, Sex of Student, and Control and Level of Institution: Selected Years, 1970 Through 2026," *Digest of Education Statistics*, February 2017, https://nces.ed.gov/programs/digest/d16/tables/dt16_303.70.asp.

33. These are not, of course, the only schools that are serious about the dropout crisis. The Education Trust reports that, between 2003 and 2013, twenty-six universities recorded double-digit gains in the campus-wide graduation rate as well as double-digit declines in the achievement gap for new-gen undergraduates. "Redesigning America's Community Colleges," a report from the Columbia University Community College Research Center, gives a shout-out to two-year colleges that have made equally impressive strides. Joseph Yeado, *Intentionally Successful: Improving Minority Student College Graduation Rates* (Washington, DC: Education Trust, July 17, 2013), https://edtrust.org/resource/intentionally-successful-improving-minority-student-college-graduation-rates/; Thomas Bailey et al., *Redesigning America's Community Colleges: A Clearer Path to Student Success* (Cambridge, MA: Harvard University Press, 2015). I've written several articles on this topic, and every time I get emails from campus leaders bragging, and with good reason, about how much progress their school is making.

CHAPTER 1

1. Fisher *v.* University of Texas, 570 U.S. 297 (2013).

2. For a summary of the argument over racial mismatch, see Mikhail Zinshteyn, "The Dispute Over Whether Attending a Good College Helps or Hurts Average Students," *The Atlantic*, March 2016, https://www.theatlantic.com/education/archive/2016/03/the-dispute-over-whether-good-colleges-help-or-hurt-average-students/475056/. UCLA law professor Richard Sander is the leading advocate of the racial mismatch theory. Richard Sander and Stuart Taylor Jr., *Mismatch: How Affirmative Action Hurts Students It's Intended to Help, and Why Universities Won't Admit It* (New York: Basic Books, 2012). In *For Discrimination: Race, Affirmative Action, and the Law* (New York: Knopf Doubleday, 2013), Harvard Law professor Randall Kennedy makes the counter-argument. In theory, "mismatch" applies to all underqualified students, though in practice it is used almost exclusively to refer to minority students.

3. Clifford Adelman, "Do We Really Have a College Access Problem?," *Change*, 2007, https://www.scribd.com/document/19810161/Do-We-Really-Have-a-College-Access-Problem.

4. On the strategies used by well-off families, see generally David L. Kirp, *Shakespeare, Einstein, and the Bottom Line: The Marketing of Higher Education* (Cambridge, MA: Harvard University Press, 2003).

5. Carolyn Hoxby and Christopher Avery, "The Missing 'One-Offs': The Hidden Supply of High-Achieving, Low Income Students," NBER Working Paper No. 18586 (December 2012); Carolyn Hoxby and Sarah Turner, *Expanding College Opportunities for High-Achieving, Low-Income Students* (Stanford, CA: Stanford Institute for Economic Policy Research, 2013), https://siepr.stanford.edu/research/publications/expanding-college-opportunities-high-achieving-low-income-students.

6. Jennifer Giancola and Richard D. Kahlenberg, *"True Merit"* (Lansdowne, VA: Jack Kent Cooke Foundation, 2016), http://www.jkcf.org/assets/1/7/JKCF_True_Merit_Report.pdf.

7. Stephen Burd, *Undermining Pell: How Colleges Compete for Wealthy Students and Leave the Low-Income Behind* (Washington, DC: New America, May 8, 2013), https://www.newamerica.org/education-policy/policy-papers/undermining-pell/.

8. "The Missing 'One-Offs': The Hidden Supply of High-Achieving, Low Income Students"; *Expanding College Opportunities for High-Achieving, Low-Income Students*.

9. Susan Dynarski et al., "Closing the Gap: The Effect of a Targeted, Tuition-Free Promise on College Choices of High-Achieving, Low-Income Students," NBER Working Paper 25349 (December 2018), http://www.nber.org/papers/w25349.

10. John Rosales, "With New Roles, School Counselors Are More Indispensable Than Ever," *NEA Today*, February 1, 2015, http://neatoday.org/2015/02/01/school-counselors-are-more-indispensable-than-ever/.

11. Benjamin L. Castleman and Lindsay C. Page, "Freshman Year Financial Aid Nudges: An Experiment to Increase FAFSA Renewal and College Persistence," *Journal of Human Resources*, vol. 51, no. 2, 389–415 (Spring 2016), http://jhr.uwpress.org/content/51/2/389.full.pdf+html.

12. Gil Press, "A Very Short History of Data Science," *Forbes*, May 28, 2013, https://www.forbes.com/sites/gilpress/2013/05/28/a-very-short-history-of-data-science/#3714a4e955cf.

13. Michael Lewis, *Moneyball: The Art of Winning an Unfair Game* (New York: Norton, 2004).

14. Charles Duhigg, "How Companies Learn Your Secrets," *The New York Times Magazine*, February 16, 2012, https://www.nytimes.com/2012/02/19/magazine/shopping-habits.html.

15. Muin J. Khoury, John P. A. Ioannidis, "Big Data Meets Public Health," *Science*, 346: 6213, 1054–1055 (November 28, 2014), http://science.sciencemag.org/content/346/6213/1054.long.

16. Jeffrey Selingo, "How Colleges Use Big Data to Target the Students They Want," *The Atlantic*, April 11, 2017, https://www.theatlantic.com/education/archive/2017/04/how-colleges-find-their-students/522516/.

17. Goldie Blumenstyk, "Blowing Off Class? We Know," *New York Times*, December 3, 2014, https://www.nytimes.com/2014/12/03/opinion/blowing-off-class-we-know.html; Libby Nelson, "Big Data 101," *Vox*, July 14, 2014, https://www.vox.com/2014/7/14/5890403/colleges-are-hoping-predictive-analytics-can-fix-their-graduation-rates; Joseph B. Treaster, "Will You Graduate? Ask Big Data," *New York Times*, February 2, 2017, https://www.nytimes.com/2017/02/02/education/edlife/will-you-graduate-ask-big-data.html; *Embracing Innovation: 2015–2016 Higher Education Industry Outlook Survey* (KPMG, 2016), http://www.kpmginstitutes.com/content/dam/kpmg/governmentinstitute/pdf/2015/he-outlook-2016.pdf; *Using Data to Improve Student Outcomes: Learning from Leading Colleges* (Washington, DC: Education Trust, May 2016), https://edtrust.org/wp-content/uploads/2014/09/HigherEdPG2_UsingDatatoImproveStudentOutcomes.pdf.

18. "Big Data 101."

19. Yonette Joseph, Mike McPhate, "Mount St. Mary's President Quits After Firings Seen as Retaliatory," *New York Times*, March 2, 2016, https://www.nytimes.com/2016/03/02/us/simon-newman-resigns-as-president-of-mount-st-marys.html.

20. "Blowing Off Class? We Know."

21. Evan Selinger, "With Big Data Invading Campus, Universities Risk Unfairly Profiling Their Students," *Christian Science Monitor*, January 13, 2015, https://www.csmonitor.com/World/Passcode/Passcode-Voices/2015/0113/With-big-data-invading-campus-universities-risk-unfairly-profiling-their-students; Mikhail Zinshteyn, "The Colleges Are Watching," *The Atlantic*, November 1, 2016, https://www.theatlantic.com/education/archive/2016/11/the-colleges-are-watching/506129/; Kayley Robsham, "Benefits of Tracking Student Involvement: What You're Missing," *Presence*, March 11, 2016, http://www.presence.io/blog/benefits-of-tracking-student-involvement-what-youre-missing/.

22. Manuela Ekowo, "Colleges Need to Use Predictive Data to Enhance—Not Hinder—Diversity," *EdSurge*, October 10, 2016, https://www.edsurge.com/news/2016-10-10-colleges-need-to-use-predictive-data-to-enhance-not-hinder-diversity.

23. Manuela Ekowo and Iris Palmer, *Predictive Analytics in Higher Education: Five Guiding Practices for Ethical Use* (Washington, DC: New America, March 6, 2017), https://www.newamerica.org/education-policy/policy-papers/predictive-analytics-higher-education/.

24. Gregory M. Walton and Geoffrey F. Cohen, "A Brief Social-Belonging Intervention Improves Academic and Health Outcomes of Minority Students," *Science,* Vol. 331, Issue 6023 (March 18, 2011), http://science.sciencemag.org/content/331/6023/1447.

This experiment was not the first to probe the impact of a brief intervention on students' academic performance. In an earlier study of minority middle-school students, Walton demonstrated that an even less intense experience could work wonders. Simply writing an essay about a personally important value, like relationships with good friends, seems to have changed attitudes toward school and, consequently, how well the essay writers did in a particular course. Only 3 percent failed the course for which they wrote the essay, compared with 11 percent of the control group. Another experiment, this one carried out by psychologists Lisa Blackwell and Kali Trzesniewski, focused on students who were predicted to do badly in middle-school math. A survey found that many of them believed their brains were fixed at birth. When they enrolled in a four-hour class about how "effortful learning" rewires the brain, they set higher goals for themselves, were more highly motivated, and more likely to think that making an effort could pay off. A year later their math grades were higher than students who hadn't learned about brain development. Lisa Blackwell, Kali H. Trzesniewski, and Carol Sorich Dweck, "Implicit Theories of Intelligence Predict Achievement Across an Adolescent Transition: A Longitudinal Study and an Intervention," *Child Development*, vol. 78, no. 1, 246–263 (January/February 2007).

25. Gregory Walton and David Yeager, "Social-Psychological Interventions in Education: They're Not Magic," *Review of Educational Research*, vol. 82, no. 2 (June, 2011), http://journals.sagepub.com/doi/abs/10.3102/0034654311405999.

26. Carol Dweck, *Mindset: The New Psychology of Success* (New York: Ballantine Books, 2006).

27. Erving Goffman, *Stigma: Notes on the Management of Spoiled Identity* (New York: Touchstone, 1963), 8.

28. Claude M. Steele and Joshua Aronson, "Stereotype Vulnerability and the Intellectual Test Performance of African-Americans," *Journal of Personality and Social Psychology*, vol. 69, 797–811 (1995). See generally Claude M. Steele, *Whistling Vivaldi: And Other Clues to How Stereotypes Affect Us* (New York: W. W. Norton, 2010).

29. "A Brief Social-Belonging Intervention Improves Academic and Health Outcomes of Minority Students."

30. "Social-Psychological Interventions in Education: They're Not Magic."

31. See, e.g., Sue Leavitt Gullo, "Using Improvement Science to Address Maternal Mortality in the US," Institute for Healthcare Improvement, April 26, 2017, http://www.ihi.org/communities/blogs/_layouts/15/ihi/community/blog/itemview.aspx?List=7d1126ec-8f63-4a3b-9926-c44ea3036813&ID=386.

32. Mikhail Zinshteyn, "Trapped in the Community College Remedial Maze," *The Atlantic*, February 26, 2016, https://www.theatlantic.com/education/archive/2016/02/community-colleges-remedial-classes/471192/.

33. Engaging students actively in problem-solving and collaborative projects produces deeper and more lasting learning than the passive experience of listening to lectures and taking notes. Kevin Eagan et al., *Undergraduate Teaching Faculty: The 2013–2014 HERI Faculty Survey* (Los Angeles: Higher Education Research Institute at University of California, Los Angeles, 2014), https://heri.ucla.edu/monographs/HERI-FAC2014-monograph.pdf.

34. Carol S. Dweck, Gregory M. Walton, and Geoffrey L. Cohen, *Academic Tenacity: Mindsets and Skills that Promote Long-Term Learning* (Seattle, WA: Gates Foundation, 2014), https://files.eric.ed.gov/fulltext/ED576649.pdf.

35. Melrose Huang, *2016–2017 Impact Report: Six Years of Results from the Carnegie Math Pathways*™ (Stanford, CA: Carnegie Foundation for the Advancement of Teaching, January 2018), https://www.carnegiefoundation.org/resources/publications/2016-2017-impact-report-six-years-of-results-from-the-carnegie-math-pathways/.

36. Uri Treisman argues that changing how college math is taught requires more than introducing pedagogical improvement. "I saw that if the work was going to scale,

faculty needed to be involved and lead it in their classrooms; administrators needed to support it; it needed to be enabled by policy. Administrative rules had to be changed, state policies had to be changed." That's the focus of his current work at the University of Texas.

37. Davis Jenkins and John Fink, *What We Know About Transfer* (New York: Community College Research Center, January 2015), https://ccrc.tc.columbia.edu/publications/what-we-know-about-transfer.html.

38. *Snapshot Report: Degree Attainment* (Herndon, VA: National Student Clearinghouse Research Center, Fall 2012), https://studentclearinghouse.info/snapshot/docs/SnapshotReport8-GradRates2-4Transfers.pdf.

39. For a superb presentation of effective strategies for reforming two-year colleges, see Thomas Bailey, Shanna Smith Jaggars, and Davis Jenkins, *Redesigning America's Community Colleges: A Clearer Path to Student Success* (Cambridge, MA: Harvard University Press, 2015).

40. Danielle Douglas-Gabriel, "Colleges Need to Do More to Help Students Transfer Credits, GAO Says," *Washington Post*, September 13, 2017, https://www.washingtonpost.com/news/grade-point/wp/2017/09/13/colleges-need-to-do-more-to-help-students-transfer-credits-gao-says/?utm_term=.d11b2553b51b; David B. Monaghan, Paul Attewell, "The Community College Route to the Bachelor's Degree," *Education Evaluation and Policy Analysis*, March 19, 2014, http://journals.sagepub.com/stoken/rbtfl/m8EKj850s9SvE/full.

The majority of these students have federal loans or Pell Grants. Both programs have eligibility limits based on the amount of time a student spends in school—twelve semesters for Pell and six years for loans. Iris Palmer, "The Student Transfer Problem and How States Can Help Solve It," *New America* blog, April 28, 2015, https://www.newamerica.org/education-policy/edcentral/student-transfer-problem/

41. https://www.insidehighered.com/views/2016/06/14/essay-challenges-community-college-students-face-transferring-earn-four-year.

42. Josh Keller, "California Is Set to Ease Path for Transfer Students," *Chronicle of Higher Education*, June 2, 2010, https://www.chronicle.com/article/California-Is-Set-to-Ease-Path/65763.

43. A report from the Community College Research Center at Columbia University, reaches the same conclusion: "Institutions could improve their transfer performance if they changed the way they serve transfer students and worked more closely with their transfer partners." Davis Jenkins and John Fink, *Tracking Transfer: New Measures of Institutional and State Effectiveness in Helping Community College Students Attain Bachelor's Degrees* (New York: Community College Research Center, 2016), https://ccrc.tc.columbia.edu/media/k2/attachments/tracking-transfer-institutional-state-effectiveness.pdf.

CHAPTER 2

1. "Top 100 Producers of Bachelor's Degrees, 2017," *Diverse Issues in Higher Education*, 2017, http://diverseeducation.com/top100/pages/BachelorsDegreeProducers2017.php.

2. Benjamin Wurmund, "How U.S. News College Rankings Promote Economic Inequality on Campus," *Politico*, September 10, 2017, https://www.politico.com/interactives/2017/top-college-rankings-list-2017-us-news-investigation/.
3. See Chapter 1 for a discussion of Claude Steele's model of stereotype vulnerability.
4. See Chapter 1 for a discussion of the "nudge" strategy.
5. Joseph Yeado et al., *Learning from High-Performing and Fast-Gaining Institutions*, (Washington, DC: Education Trust, 2014), https://edtrust.org/wp-content/uploads/2013/10/PracticeGuide1.pdf.
6. Sara Goldrick-Rab, "It's Hard to Study When You're Hungry," *New York Times*, January 14, 2018, https://www.nytimes.com/2018/01/14/opinion/hunger-college-food-insecurity.html; Elizabeth A. Harris, "Behind the Problem of Student Homelessness," *New York Times*, April 7, 2017, https://www.nytimes.com/2017/04/07/education/edlife/college-student-homelessness.html.
7. See Chapter 1 for a discussion of the belonging and mindset models.
8. Donna Tamm and Amy Scott, "Top College Students Who Lose Small Amounts of Financial Aid More Likely to Drop Out," *Marketplace*, November 2, 2016, https://www.marketplace.org/2016/11/01/education/students-who-lose-financial-aid-are-more-likely-drop-out-study-says.
9. Sandy Baum and Saul Schwartz, *Student Aid, Student Behavior, and Educational Attainment* (Washington, DC: George Washington University, September 2013), https://gsehd.gwu.edu/sites/default/files/documents/PUBLISHED_Baum_Schwartz.pdf.
10. See generally Ellen Schrecker, *The Lost Soul of Higher Education* (New York: New Press, 2010).
11. Scott Freeman et al., "Active learning increases student performance in science, engineering, and mathematics," *Proceedings of the National Academy of Sciences*, 111 (23): 8410–8415 (June 10, 2014), http://www.pnas.org/content/111/23/8410.
12. Jeff Selingo et al., *The Next Generation University* (Washington, DC: New America, 2013), https://static.newamerica.org/attachments/2318-the-next-generation-university/Next_Generation_University_FINAL_FOR_RELEASE.8897220087ff4bd6afe8f6682594e3b0.pdf.
13. The University Innovation Alliance, 2018, http://www.theuia.org/#about.
14. "How U.S. News college rankings promote economic inequality on campus."

CHAPTER 3

1. "Signature 12 Supplement: Completing College: A National View of Student Attainment Rates by Race and Ethnicity—Fall 2010 Cohort," https://nscresearchcenter.org/signaturereport12-supplement-2/
2. Xianglei Chen and Sean Simone, *Remedial Coursetaking at U.S. Public 2- and 4-Year Institutions: Scope, Experiences, and Outcomes* (Washington, DC: National Center for Education Statistics, September 2016), https://nces.ed.gov/pubs2016/2016405.pdf.
3. Previously, 80 percent of the students failed one or more of the assessment exams. In fall 2017, changes in CUNY placement policies and an increase in retesting and test prep offerings led to a decline in remediation rates to 65 percent. Other

strategies, such as increasingly placing students into a math pathway, like statistics, aligned to their major, expansion of co-requisite remedial offerings, and expansion and increased use of pre-matriculation programs like CUNY Start contributed to the decrease in the number of students having to take remedial classes.

4. *Report of the CUNY Task Force on Developmental Education* (New York: CUNY Task Force on Developmental Education, June 1, 2016), http://www2.cuny. edu/wp-content/uploads/sites/4/page-assets/about/administration/offices/ undergraduate-studies/developmental-education/Proposed-Recommendations-of-RTF-06.17.16.final.pdf.

5. CUNY Start also offers a part-time program to students who fail all three skills areas but may not be able to do the FT program 25 hours/week.

6. See Chapter 1 for a discussion of Statway.

7. See Chapter 2 for a discussion of belonging and mindset.

8. Sean Trainor, "How Community Colleges Changed the Whole Idea of Education in America," *Time*, October 20, 2015, http://time.com/4078143/community-college-history/.

9. For a comprehensive description of ASAP, see Diana Strumbos, Donna Linderman, and Carson C. Hicks, "Postsecondary Pathways Out of Poverty: City University of New York Accelerated Study in Associate Programs and the Case for National Policy," *RSF: The Russell Sage Foundation Journal of the Social Sciences* 4, no. 3, 100–117 (2018), https://www.rsfjournal.org/doi/full/10.7758/RSF.2018.4.3.06

10. ASAP has expanded quickly, and the goal is to offer the program to all students.

11. "Tuition-Free Degree Program: The Excelsior Scholarship," New York State, https:// www.ny.gov/programs/tuition-free-degree-program-excelsior-scholarship. To be eligible, a student must attend a school in the CUNY or SUNY system.

12. Paul Fain, "Full-Time Finishers," *Inside Higher Ed*, April 19, 2017, https://www. insidehighered.com/news/2017/04/19/students-who-attend-college-full-time-even-one-semester-are-more-likely-graduate.

13. Paul Fain, "Back of the Line," *Inside Higher Ed*, May 29, 2012, https://www. insidehighered.com/news/2012/05/29/law-may-contribute-advising-overload-californias-community-colleges.

14. See generally Diana Strumbos and Zineta Kolenovic, *Six-Year Outcomes of ASAP Students: Transfer and Degree Attainment* (New York: City University of New York, January 2017), http://www1.cuny.edu/sites/asap/wp-content/uploads/sites/8/ 2017/01/201701_ASAP_Eval_Brief_Six_Year_Outcomes_FINAL.pdf.

15. Diana Strumbos and Zineta Kolenovic, *ASAP Graduation Rates by Race/Ethnicity, Gender and Pell Status* (New York: City University of New York, September 2016), http://www.sheeo.org/sites/default/files/201609_ASAP_Eval_Brief_ Subgroups_FINAL.pdf; "Six-Year Outcomes of ASAP Students: Transfer and Degree Attainment."

16. Susan Scrivener et al., *Doubling Graduation Rates: Three-Year Effects of CUNY's Accelerated Study in Associate Programs (ASAP) for Developmental Education Students"* (New York: MDRC, 2015), https://www.mdrc.org/publication/doubling-graduation-rates.

17. Henry Levin and Emma Garcia, *Benefit-Cost Analysis of Accelerated Study in Associate Programs (ASAP) of the City University of New York (CUNY)* (New York: Center for

Benefit-Cost Studies in Education, Teachers College, Columbia University, 2011), http://www1.nyc.gov/assets/opportunity/pdf/Levin_ASAP_Benefit_Cost_ Report_FINAL_05212013.pdf; Henry Levin and Emma Garcia, *Cost-effectiveness of Accelerated Study in Associate Programs (ASAP) of the City University of New York (CUNY)* (New York: Center for Benefit-Cost Studies in Education, Teachers College, Columbia University, 2011), http://www1.cuny.edu/sites/asap/wp-content/uploads/sites/8/2014/06/Levin-ASAP-Cost-Effectiveness-Report.pdf.

18. Derek Bok, *The Struggle to Reform Our Colleges* (Princeton, NJ: Princeton University Press, 2017).

19. CUNY is not, of course, the only successful community college system. See generally "The Aspen Prize for Community College Excellence," Aspen Institute, http:// highered.aspeninstitute.org/aspen-prize/. Valencia College, which is discussed in Chapter 5, was the first winner of the prize, and Hostos Community College was a finalist in 2015.

20. "Ohio Programs Based on CUNY's Accelerated Study in Associate Programs (ASAP) More Than Double Graduation Rates: Rare Example of a Program Model Being Successfully Adapted in a Different Setting," MDRC (December 2018), https://www.mdrc.org/news/press-release/ohio-programs-based-cuny-s-accelerated-study-associate-programs-asap-more-double.

21. Donna Y. Ford, "Segregation and the Underrepresentation of Blacks and Hispanics in Gifted Education," *Roeper Review*, 143–154 (June 24, 2014), https://www.tandfonline.com/doi/full/10.1080/02783193.2014.919563.

22. A review of the literature on student support services concludes that students whose advisers helped them with both personal and academic issues were more likely to finish college. Melinda Mechur Karp and Georgia West Stacey, *What We Know About Academic Supports* (New York: Community College Research Center, September 2013), http://ccrc.tc.columbia.edu/media/k2/attachments/what-we-know-about-nonacademic-student-supports.pdf.

CHAPTER 4

1. This section draws on conversations with Angel Sanchez, as well as articles published in the Valencia and UCF magazines. Rachel Williams, "Prison to Law School: How Education Turned a Former Gang Member's Life Around," *UCF Today*, May 2, 2017, https://today.ucf.edu/how-education-turned-a-former-gang-members-life-around/; "Angel Sanchez—An Incredible Journey: Valencia's Distinguished Graduate Goes from Prison to Honors College," *Valencia College*, March 27, 2017, https://medium.com/valencia-college/angel-sanchez-an-incredible-journey-valencias-distinguished-graduate-goes-from-prison-to-honors-fa06f82b4374.

2. "2017 College Rankings," *Washington Monthly*, September/October 2017, http:// wmf.washingtonmonthly.com/college_guide/2017/WM_2017_Embargoed_ Rankings.pdf.

3. Hitt isn't concerned about how long it takes the transfer students to graduate. "They're working, they have family responsibilities—why should it matter if they need an extra year or two?" This stance sits poorly with the politicians in Tallahassee, who want these students in and out the door, BA in hand, in four years,

two at the community college and two at the university. It is also inconsistent with research showing that part-time students are less likely to graduate, the evidence base that CUNY's community college leaders relied on in insisting that the students in its degree-boosting associate degree program, called ASAP, take a full course load. "Even One Semester" (Center for Community College Engagement, 2017), http://www.ccsse.org/nr2017/. The president points to the UCF data, which tells a different story—by their sixth year at UCF, having previously spent three or four years at community college, they're as likely to graduate as students who came to UCF straight out of high school.

4. Nick Anderson, "Is Bigger Better? 54,000 Students and Growing, U. Of Central Florida Storms Higher Ed.," *Washington Post*, September 20, 2015, https://www.washingtonpost.com/local/education/with-54000-students-and-growing-u-of-central-florida-storms-higher-ed/2015/09/20/0db73380-4cbd-11e5-bfb9-9736d04fc8e4_story.html?utm_term=.bc8d65040d6e.

5. Sanford Shugart et al., "Valencia's Big Ideas: Sustaining Authentic Organizational Change Through Shared Purpose and Culture" (Orlando, FL: Valencia College, 2018), https://valenciacollege.edu/ournextbigidea/qep.cfm.

6. This section is adapted from Valencia College, "Mission, Vision, and Strategy," https://valenciacollege.edu/academic-affairs/institutional-effectiveness-planning/strategic-plan/goals.cfm.

7. "Valencia's Big Ideas: Sustaining Authentic Organizational Change through Shared Purpose and Culture."

8. The touchstone is Diane Halpern (Ed.), *Changing College Classrooms* (New York: Jossey-Bass, 1994).

9. Meredith Kalodner, "Why Are Graduation Rates at Community Colleges So Low?," *The Hechinger Report*, May 15, 2015, http://hechingerreport.org/new-book-addresses-low-community-college-graduation-rates/. See generally Thomas Bailey, Shanna Smith Jaggers, and Davis Jenkins, *Redesigning America's Community Colleges: A Clearer Path to Student Success* (Cambridge, MA: Harvard University Press, 2015).

10. Shugart et al., "Valencia's Big Ideas: Sustaining Authentic Organizational Change through Shared Purpose and Culture."

11. Students who excel academically have a chance to do research with their professors, and as the spring 2017 semester wound down, they showed off their work at a jam-packed poster session. Events like this are a staple of academic conferences, but few colleges let undergraduates present their work this way. Gunika Datt was exploring a putative vaccine candidate for Zika virus: "Given the availability of viral isolate sequences, we hypothesized structural protein conservation would highlight ideal universal vaccine targets." Aimee Klaschus was studying freshwater biodiversity, "vital to the survival of freshwater ecosystems, yet an underrepresented field in ecology." And Faith Patchett was analyzing how the bond between patient and psychotherapist altered the outcome of occupational therapy. These students, like most of their classmates at the poster session, had a PhD and a research career in their sights.

12. Jason Shafrin, "94% of College Professors Are Above Average," *Healthcare Economist*, April 11, 2008, http://healthcare-economist.com/2008/04/11/94-of-college-professors-are-above-average/.

13. Linda Shrieves Beaty, "Valencia Ranks 4th in Nation for Number of Associate Degrees," *Valencia College*, October 12, 2016, http://news.valenciacollege.edu/about-valencia/valencia-ranks-4th-in-nation-for-number-of-associate-degrees-4/.

14. Faculty salaries are low—especially for part-time faculty, who teach about half of the classes—and teaching loads are high.

15. "Highest Rated Junior and Community Colleges of 2016–2017," *Rate My Professor*, http://www.ratemyprofessors.com/blog/toplist/highest-rated-junior-and-community-colleges-of-2016-2017.

16. On the rising cost of higher education, see Robert Archibald and David Feldman, *Why Does Higher Education Cost So Much?* (Oxford: Oxford University Press, 2011).

    "Baumol's Cost Disease, posited by the late Princeton economist William Baumol, notes that higher education is a service that is highly labor-intensive, and which requires skilled labor in particular. And in recent decades, the cost of skilled labor has shot upwards relative to the cost of unskilled labor; in other words, college graduates started to pull away from their high-school educated peers. So it should come as no surprise that colleges would see costs rise. The cost of their main input, people, was rising a lot. The cost of college has increased at about the same rate as other skill-intensive services." Dylan Matthews, "The Tuition Is Too Damn High, Part V—Is the Economy Forcing Colleges to Spend More?," *Washington Post*, August 30, 2013, https://www.washingtonpost.com/news/wonk/wp/2013/08/30/the-tuition-is-too-damn-high-part-v-is-the-economy-forcing-colleges-to-spend-more/?noredirect=on&utm_term=.3268be31cd8a; William Baumol, "Health Care, Education and The Cost Disease: A Looming Crisis for Public Choice," *Public Choice* 77, no. 17 (September 1993).

17. John Immerwahr, Jean Johnson, and Paul Gasbarra, *The Iron Triangle* (New York, NY: National Center for Public Policy and Higher Education and Public Agenda, 2008), http://www.highereducation.org/reports/iron_triangle/IronTriangle.pdf.

18. "The Best of the Best: The Rise of the Ivy League," *Niche*, March 1, 2014, https://ink.niche.com/rise-of-the-ivy-league/.

19. College football fans may recall that UCF won the Fiesta Bowl in 2014, the biggest upset in the history of that bowl game.

20. "Is Bigger Better? 54,000 Students and Growing, U. Of Central Florida Storms Higher Ed."

21. David L. Kirp, *Shakespeare, Einstein, and the Bottom Line: The Marketing of Higher Education* (Cambridge, MA: Harvard University Press, 2003).

22. Eric Bettinger and Susanna Loeb, "Promises and Pitfalls of Online Education," *Evidence Speaks Reports* (Washington, DC: Brookings Institution, 2017), https://www.brookings.edu/wp-content/uploads/2017/06/ccf_20170609_loeb_evidence_speaks1.pdf.

23. Martin Kurzweil and Jessie Brown, "Breaking the Iron Triangle at the University of Central Florida" (New York: Ithaka S+R, August 26, 2015), http://www.sr.ithaka.org/publications/breaking-the-iron-triangle-at-the-university-of-central-florida/.

24. Faculty need to be convinced to start teaching online. "Professors are busy with other things," Tom Cavanaugh notes. "It's unfair for me to say, 'I've got cool software that will help your students' and expect them to use it—they don't have the

bandwidth. I need to buy space in their lives—summer salaries, assurances that this work counts for tenure and promotion—if they're going to innovate."

This work consumes a great deal of time that could otherwise be spent doing the kind of research that counts when it comes to tenure and promotion. But UCF professors don't necessarily have to choose between designing a course and writing a journal article, because each activity counts when a professor's work is being evaluated.

25. "The Start of Something Big: How a Moment of Creative Inspiration Has Fueled President John C. Hitt's 25-Year Tenure At UCF," *Pegasus* (n.d.), https://www.ucf.edu/pegasus/start-something-big/.

26. The unweighted scale is most common, and the highest-possible GPA on this scale is a 4.0. The unweighted scale doesn't take the *difficulty* of classes, such as advanced placement courses, into account. Weighted scales are used at many high schools. Typically, they go up to a 5.0.

27. The conference, sponsored by the Aspen Institute, is described in greater detail in Chapter 8.

28. A 2013 performance by Sandy Shugart's band can be found on YouTube. https://www.youtube.com/watch?v=xLGAyAM0o00

29. "Building Seamless Degree Pathways in Florida," *Higher Education Transformation* (Seattle, WA: Gates Foundation, 2014), http://postsecondary.gatesfoundation.org/wp-content/uploads/2014/11/Case-Study-Valencia_FINAL.pdf.

30. Saundra Amrhein, "Where Dreams Come True," *Politico*, June 18, 2015, https://www.politico.com/magazine/story/2015/06/orlando-what-works-119159.

31. Sophie Quinton, "Why Central Florida Kids Choose Community College," *The Atlantic*, February 10, 2014, https://www.theatlantic.com/politics/archive/2014/02/why-central-florida-kids-choose-community-college/430605/.

32. See Chapter 3 for a discussion of the Georgia State model.

CHAPTER 5

1. Mitch Smith, "Longhorns Who Take Too Long," *Inside Higher Ed.*, February 16, 2012, https://www.insidehighered.com/news/2012/02/16/texas-wants-boost-four-year-graduation-rate-20-points.

2. Tamar Lewin, "Most College Students Don't Earn a Degree in 4 Years, Study Finds," *New York Times*, December 2, 2014, https://www.nytimes.com/2014/12/02/education/most-college-students-dont-earn-degree-in-4-years-study-finds.html.

3. National Student Clearinghouse Research Center, "Snapshot Report—Persistence and Retention," May 3, 2016, https://nscresearchcenter.org/snapshotreport-persistenceretention22/.

4. Because of enrollment constraints at UT Austin, that figure was subsequently reduced to the top 7 percent; at other public universities in the state it remains 10 percent.

5. Matthew Watkins, "System Chancellor McRaven Blasts Top Ten Percent Rule," *Texas Tribune*, January 21, 2016, https://www.texastribune.org/2016/01/21/ut-system-chancellor-mcraven-blasts-top-ten-percen/.

6. Latino students have been the main beneficiaries of the 10 percent rule. The percentage of black students has barely budged, and the percentage of white students has declined.
7. "Snapshot Report—Persistence and Retention."
8. Smaller UT colleges, which don't have enough students to mount such a program, send their undergraduates to campus-wide programs operated by the Division of Diversity and Community Engagement.
9. Claude Steele and Joshua Aronson, "Stereotype threat and the intellectual test performance of African-Americans," *Journal of Personality and Social Psychology* 69, 797–811 (November 1995), https://www.ncbi.nlm.nih.gov/pubmed/7473032. See Chapter 2 for a discussion of the growth mindset and belonging models.
10. As is the case with most such studies, the university is identified only as a flagship school, but David Yeager and David Laude confirm that it was conducted at UT.
11. David Yeager et al., "Teaching a Lay Theory Before College Narrows Achievement Gaps at Scale," *Proceedings of the National Academy of Sciences of the United States of America* 113, no. 24, E3341–E3348 (June 4, 2016), https://www.ncbi.nlm.nih.gov/pubmed/27247409.
12. "Stereotype Threat and The Intellectual Test Performance of African-Americans."
13. Uri Treisman, who helped to develop Statway, is a UT professor. He is asking the same kind of question, though from a broader perspective: "How do we take advances in economics, organizational theory, learning theory, informational sciences and incorporate them into instruction in a way that profoundly impacts students? There are a lot of wonderful teachers who're passionate about teaching and learning, who can make a big difference in the lives of anywhere from 30–100 students. That's not what we're talking about, we're talking about society. That's why I spend so much time with my students', as well as David [Yeager]'s and Carol [Dweck]'s. I want to figure out what we can build into pedagogy."
14. Laude describes his approach in a 2014 TED Talk, "Everyone Can Get an A:" https://www.youtube.com/watch?v=WQ82Uukl6rg.
15. Gregory L. Fenves, "2017 State of the University Address," University of Texas at Austin, September 12, 2017, https://president.UTexas.edu/2017-state-university-address.

CHAPTER 6

1. This section draws on Alejandra Marchevsky and Jean Theoharis, *Not Working Latina Immigrants, Low-Wage Jobs, and the Failure of Welfare Reform* (New York: New York University Press, 2006).
2. "New Report Shows Long Beach College Promise Has Produced Significant Gains in Student Achievement," *LA Sentinel*, April 2, 2018. https://lasentinel.net/new-report-shows-long-beach-college-promise-has-produced-significant-gains-in-student-achievement.html.
3. Lillian Mongeau, "The Long Beach Miracle," *The Atlantic*, February 2, 2016, https://www.theatlantic.com/education/archive/2016/02/the-long-beach-miracle/459315/.

4. "Economic Diversity and Student Outcomes at California State University, Long Beach." *New York Times, The Upshot,* https://www.nytimes.com/interactive/projects/college-mobility/california-state-university-long-beach?mcubz=3.

5. "Best Global Universities," *U.S. News and World Report: Education,* https://www.usnews.com/education/best-global-universities.

6. "Dowell's Legacy All About Student Success," *Long Beach State University, Office of Public Affairs Newsroom,* May 16, 2016, http://web.csulb.edu/newsroom/dowells-legacy-all-about-student-success/.

7. Mary C. Murphy and Gregory M. Walton, "From Prejudiced People to Prejudiced Places: A Social-Contextual Approach to Prejudice," in Charles Stangor and Christian Crandall (Eds.), *Stereotyping and Prejudice* (London: Psychology Press, 2017).

8. Hiroyuki Yamada and Anthony Bryk, "Assessing the First Two Years of Statway" (Stanford, CA: Carnegie Foundation for the Advancement of Teaching, 2016), https://www.carnegiefoundation.org/wp-content/uploads/2016/06/Assessing_Statway_Effectiveness2016.pdf.

CHAPTER 7

1. This section draws on interviews with administrators, faculty, and students. Cullen Murphy, "Home: Some Thoughts on the Frost Library Protest," *Amherst Magazine,* Summer 2016, https://www.amherst.edu/amherst-story/magazine/issues/2016-summer/home provides a nuanced account of these events.

2. "President Martin's Statement on Campus Protests," Amherst College, November 15, 2015, https://www.amherst.edu/amherst-story/president/statements/node/620480.

3. William Tyler, *A History of Amherst College* (New York: F. H. Hitchcock, 1894); Noah Webster, "Transcript of the Manuscript History of Amherst College," Amherst College, 1834, https://www.amherst.edu/library/archives/exhibitions/webster/transcription.

4. "Kennedy Documents," Amherst College, Fall 1963, https://www.amherst.edu/library/archives/exhibitions/kennedy/documents.

5. This material is collected in "Amherst Reacts," http://digital-scholarship-2016.wordpress.amherst.edu/amherst-protests/black-student-protests/admissions/.

6. In addition to interviews, this section draws on "Campus Revolutionary," *Bloomberg Business Week,* February 26, 2006, https://www.bloomberg.com/news/articles/2006-02-26/campus-revolutionary; and David Zax, "Wanted: Smart Students from Poor Families," *Yale Alumni Magazine,* January/February 2014, https://yalealumnimagazine.com/articles/3801-wanted-smart-students-from-poor-families.

7. "Campus Revolutionary."

8. William Bowen et al., *Equity and Excellence in American Higher Education* (Charlottesville: University of Virginia Press, 2005).

9. David Leonhardt, "Top Colleges, Largely for the Elite," *New York Times,* May 25, 2011, https://www.nytimes.com/2011/05/25/business/economy/25leonhardt.html.

10. Donald Heller, *Pell Grant Recipients in Selective Colleges and Universities* (New York: The Century Foundation, 2003), http://theunbrokenwindow.com/Higher%20Ed/Higher%20Ed%20Course/pellgrantheller.pdf.

11. "Home: Some Thoughts on the Frost Library Protest."

12. Rachel B. Rubin, "Recruiting, Redefining, and Recommitting: The Quest to Increase Socioeconomic Diversity at Amherst College," *Equity & Excellence in Education*, vol. 44, no. 4, 512–531 (2011).

13. "National Liberal Arts Colleges," *U.S. News & World Report: Best Colleges Rankings*, 2018, https://www.usnews.com/best-colleges/rankings/national-liberal-arts-colleges "2017 College Rankings," *Washington Monthly*, September/October 2017, http://wmf.washingtonmonthly.com/college_guide/2017/WM_2017_Embargoed_Rankings.pdf.

14. See David Leonhardt, "New Prize Rewards Economic Diversity at Colleges," *New York Times*, April 7, 2015, https://www.nytimes.com/2015/04/07/upshot/07up-leonhardt.html, and David Leonhardt, "Top Colleges Doing the Most for the American Dream," *New York Times*, May 25, 2017, https://www.nytimes.com/interactive/2017/05/25/sunday-review/opinion-pell-table.html. See also William Bowen and Derek Bok, *The Shape of the River* (Princeton, NJ: Princeton University Press, 1999); William Bowen and Martin Kurzweil, *Equity and Excellence in American Higher Education* (Princeton, NJ: Princeton University Press, 2006).

15. Stephanie Reitz, "Amherst Picks New President," *Boston Globe*, June 15, 2011, http://archive.boston.com/news/education/higher/articles/2011/06/15/amherst_college_picks_new_president/.

16. Cathy Pierre, "How Much Do You Study? Apparently 17 Hours a Week Is the Norm," *USA Today*, August 8, 2014, http://college.usatoday.com/2014/08/18/how-much-do-you-study-apparently-17-hours-a-week-is-the-norm/.

17. Andy Rosen, "Amherst College Program Helps New Students to Adapt," *Boston Globe*, January 2, 2017, https://www.bostonglobe.com/metro/2017/01/01/acclimating-amherst-college-after-orientation-ends/JniVmj50FCPt1tHC7V8fbP/story.html.

18. "Advice for New Students from Those Who Know (Older Students)," *New York Times*, August 2, 2015, https://www.nytimes.com/2015/08/02/education/edlife/advice-for-new-students-from-those-who-know-old-students.html.

CHAPTER 8

1. David L. Kirp, "An Honors College That Honors Grit," *New York Times*, May 22, 2018, https://www.nytimes.com/2018/05/22/opinion/honors-college-rutgers.html; David Von Drehle, "The Ten Best College Presidents," *Time*, November 11, 2009, http://content.time.com/time/specials/packages/article/0,28804,1937938_1937933_1937920,00.html.

2. Surveying schools that punch beyond their weight, the Education Trust concluded that "it matters a lot whether campus leaders make student success a top institution-wide priority—and when they stick with that priority over multiple years." Kevin Carey, *Choosing to Improve* (Washington, DC: Education Trust, 2005), https://1k9gl1yevnfp2lpq1dhrqe17-wpengine.netdna-ssl.com/wp-content/uploads/2013/10/Choosing_to_improve.pdf.

3. Joshua Bolkan, "University Innovation Alliance Boosts Low-Income Grads 25 Percent," *Campus Technology*, September 27, 2017, https://campustechnology.com/articles/2017/09/27/university-innovation-alliance-boosts-lowincome-grads-25-percent.aspx.

4. Remedial math is the exception to this hands-off posture, but those courses are seen as a service that most institutions would happily rid themselves of.

5. Benjamin Wermund, "How U.S. News College Rankings Promote Economic Inequality on Campus," *Politico*, September 10, 2017, https://www.politico.com/interactives/2017/top-college-rankings-list-2017-us-news-investigation/.

6. Michael D. Cohen, James G. March, and Johan P. Olsen, "A Garbage Can Model of Organizational Choice," *Administrative Science Quarterly* 17, no. 1, 1–25 (March 1972).

7. "Too often, presidents avoid risk by largely maintaining existing budget allocations, fearful that reallocating funds might cost people jobs or otherwise upset the status quo," the Aspen Institute notes, in a 2012 report. "Exceptional presidents minimize risk by tying controversial funding decisions to shared goals, often embedded in strategic plans. They understand that budget reallocations are necessary to maximize the portion of limited resources spent on what matters most to student success and to make clear that the bottom line—where dollars are spent—will be guided first and foremost by the institution's student access and success mission. *Crisis and Opportunity: Aligning the Community College Presidency with Student Success*" (Washington, DC: Aspen Institute, 2012), https://assets.aspeninstitute.org/content/uploads/files/content/upload/CEP_Final_Report.pdf.

8. David L. Kirp, "When Your College Has Your Back," *New York Times*, March 2, 2018, https://www.nytimes.com/2018/03/02/opinion/sunday/graduation-rates-wayne-state.html.

INDEX